Essential Lives

# Bill Gates

Essential Lives

# Bill Gates

by Ruth Strother

**Content Consultant**
David Bauder
National writer, Associated Press

ABDO
Publishing Company

# CREDITS

Published by ABDO Publishing Company, 8000 West 78th Street, Edina, Minnesota 55439. 

Printed in the United States.

Editor: Jill Sherman
Cover Design: Becky Daum
Interior Design: Lindaanne Donohoe

**Library of Congress Cataloging-in-Publication Data**
Strother, Ruth.
Bill Gates / Ruth Strother.
p. cm. — (Essential lives)
Includes bibliographical references and index.
ISBN 978-1-59928-841-3
1. Gates, Bill, 1955—Juvenile literature. 2. Businessmen—United States—Biography—Juvenile literature. 3. Computer software industry—United States—History—Juvenile literature. 4. Microsoft Corporation—History—Juvenile literature. I. Title.

HD9696.63.U62G377 2008
338.7'610053092—dc22 [B]

2007012269

# TABLE OF CONTENTS

Chapter 1

The Altair 8800 was the first personal computer.

# Project Breakthrough

One freezing day in December, Bill Gates and his friend, Paul Allen, saw the January 1975 issue of *Popular Electronics* magazine. On the cover was a picture of the Altair 8800 with the words "Project Breakthrough! World's First Minicomputer Kit to Rival Commercial Models ..." The two looked at each other and knew that this was it. They had been working together on computers since high school. The Altair 8800 was something entirely new. They were on the brink of a new era, in which there would be "a computer on every desk and in every home."[1]

Computers were very different in the early 1970s than they are today. One computer could cost millions of dollars and completely fill a room. The computer Gates and his friends used at Lakeside School was a GE-owned timesharing teletype system. The school had a teletype machine, which was connected to a phone line. By typing a command into the teletype, it would "talk" to an off-site program data processor (PDP) through the phone line. Every time this system was used, a fee was charged.

The Altair 8800, in contrast, was small enough to fit on a desktop. It contained its own data processor. The Altair was clearly a breakthrough in computer technology. When Gates and Allen saw the Altair, they knew they were looking at a new type of computer.

**The Altair Prototype**

Before the January 1975 issue of *Popular Electronics* came out, the magazine's technical editor wanted to test the Altair. The manufacturer sent him the initial prototype of the Altair, the only one in existence, by train. It never arrived. Somehow, it was lost in transit. Another prototype could not be made in time, so the magazine constructed a look-alike, and that is what appeared on the cover.

## Opportunity Knocks

The Altair 8800 was the first personal computer (PC), and it was revolutionary. It had been developed around a microchip, the tiny data processor in a computer, called the Intel 8080. But it was still missing something very important. The Altair was a kit, and it was of interest mainly to hobbyists. You could build it, but you could not do much else with it. No one had developed software that could be used with the Altair 8800—at least not yet.

Fearing that computers would explode into the world without them, Gates called MITS (Micro Instrumentation and Telemetry Systems), the manufacturer of the Altair 8800. He told its owner, Ed Roberts, that he had a BASIC program that could be used with the Altair. By that time, MITS had heard from a lot of people making such claims. They were all told that whoever crossed the MITS threshold first with a working program would get the deal. Gates and Allen followed up their phone call with a letter.

**Naming the Altair**

No one knew what to call the Altair until the 12-year-old daughter of the technical editor of *Popular Electronics* suggested the name. She had been watching a *Star Trek* episode in which the Enterprise was adventuring to the star Altair.

BASIC, short for beginner's all-purpose symbolic instruction code, was one of the handful of high-level languages used for programming a computer at that time. As its name suggests, it was one of the more simple programming languages. Before BASIC, FORTRAN was the computer language of choice. In the 1960s, Dartmouth College had a computer system available for all of its student body to use, but it was too complicated for most people. Two Dartmouth professors took it upon themselves to develop the BASIC language. BASIC allowed computers to become accessible beyond universities and the government.

The GE system Gates and Allen had used in high school had run on BASIC. The two had spent many hours studying manuals and teaching themselves the language. The ever-competitive and confident Gates skipped his classes and weekly poker games in order to write the program that he claimed he had already written. There was one problem: neither Allen nor Gates had an Altair to test their BASIC program. But as long as they understood the Intel 8080 chip inside and out, Gates could write the program. So they bought the chip's manual. As Gates worked almost around the clock writing code, Allen searched for a computer he could use to simulate the Altair. This is what they would use to test Gates's BASIC program.

## Moment of Truth

Gates and Allen frantically worked for two months writing, testing, and perfecting their BASIC program. They did not have the Intel 8080 chip, and they did not have the Altair microcomputer. What they had was drive, smarts, and confidence.

Allen was scheduled to fly to Albuquerque, New Mexico, where the MITS offices were located. The night before the trip, Gates stayed up rereading the manual to make sure he had understood everything perfectly. When he decided that his code was free of errors, he punched it out on

### Flipping Pancakes

In 1975, an issue of the *American Mathematical Monthly* came out with an article introducing a problem that had stumped everyone at Harvard. The article was written by Jacob E. Goodman, but he used the name Harry Dweighter. Here it is as it originally appeared:

> *The chef in our place is sloppy, and when he prepares a stack of pancakes they come out all different sizes. Therefore, when I deliver them to a customer, on the way to the table I rearrange them (so that the smallest winds up on top, and so on, down to the largest at the bottom) by grabbing several from the top and flipping them over, repeating this (varying the number I flip) as many times as necessary. If there are n pancakes, what is the maximum number of flips (as a function f(n) of n) that I will ever have to use to rearrange them?*[2]

Gates was sure he could solve the problem. He thought it was much like designing algorithms to solve problems. Professor Christos Papadimitriou, who worked at that time in Harvard's computer science department, helped Gates solve the problem. Years later, they added a twist: the pancakes were burned on one side and the problem had to be solved with the burned side down.

the paper tape that was to be fed into the Altair. The next day, he handed it over to Allen.

Allen boarded the plane with a BASIC program that was unproven. He knew that even one little error in the code could sabotage the entire project. Suddenly, he realized that he and Gates had not written the bootstrap program that needed to be keyed into the Altair so it would know how to load BASIC. In a mad rush, Allen wrote the program, finishing it just before the plane landed.

Meeting Allen at the airport in a pick-up truck was a casually dressed Ed Roberts. They went straight to the MITS office, which was far different than the corporate environment Allen had been expecting. On top of that disappointment, he had to wait until the next day before giving his demonstration.

The next day finally came. That morning, Allen fed the BASIC tape into the Altair, keyed in the loading

**BASIC Manual**

Dartmouth's first BASIC manual opens with easy-to-understand language to describe the importance of accuracy in a program: "A program is a set of directions, a recipe, that is used to provide an answer to some problem. It usually consists of a set of instructions to be performed or carried out in a certain order. It starts with the given data and parameters as the ingredients, and ends up with a set of answers as the cake. And, as with ordinary cakes, if you make a mistake in your program, you will end up with something else—perhaps hash!"[3]

program, stood back, and held his breath.

Gates had written this BASIC program for a computer that he had never seen. This was the first time it was being run on the computer for which it was written. Would the loading code that Allen had written on the plane work? Had Gates made any mistakes? Would their BASIC program work? The outcome would help set the stage for the building of one of the largest and most successful companies in the history of the United States.

**Hewlett Packard**

David Packard and Bill Hewlett founded Hewlett Packard in 1939. Although their first product, HP 200A, was of interest primarily to engineers, it caught the eye of Walt Disney Pictures. They used the revised HP200B to help create the highly acclaimed animated film *Fantasia*.

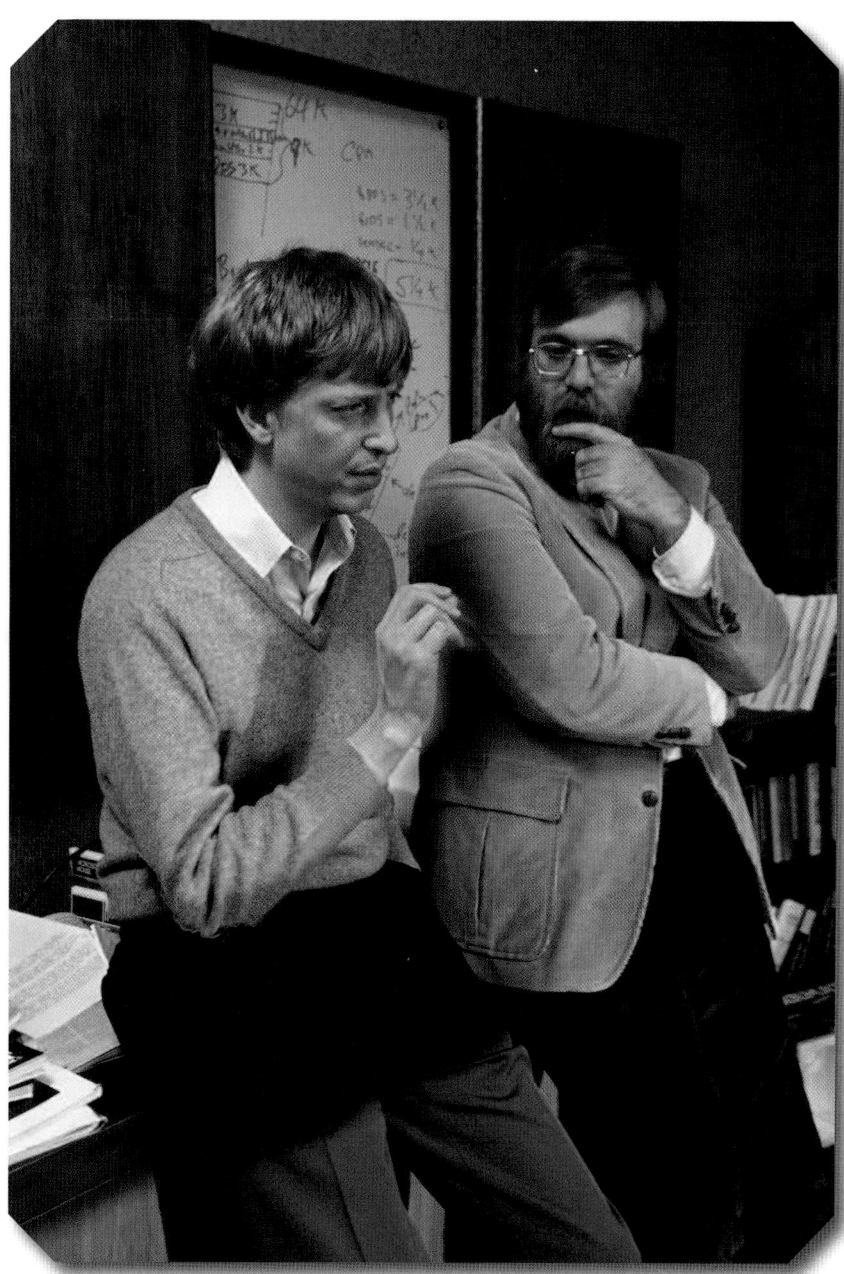

*Bill Gates (left) and Paul Allen (right) began their careers by writing computer software.*

Chapter 2

*William H. Gates Jr. with his son Bill Gates*

# The People Who Shaped the Man

Bill Gates went on to become a great success. But he did not get to the brink of the personal computer revolution that day in 1975 all by himself. His family had a lot to do with developing the man Bill Gates would become.

The Gates family was close-knit, ambitious, and competitive—traits that Bill Gates has exhibited throughout his life.

## Family History

William H. Gates Jr. (Bill Gates's father was actually born William Gates III but legally changed his name to Jr. during World War II) was born in 1927 in Bremerton, Washington, where his father owned a furniture store. He enrolled in the University of Washington, where he earned his bachelor's and law degrees. He was the first in his family to graduate from college. He then moved back home to work as an assistant city attorney. He later married his college sweetheart, Mary Maxwell.

Mary Maxwell was born in Seattle, Washington, in 1929. She came from a family of bankers and politicians who were wealthy and active in Seattle's high society. Her grandfather, James Willard Maxwell, was a well-respected banker. He served on the boards of the Seattle Chamber of

**What's in a Name?**

A man named after his father will have the suffix Junior (Jr.) added to his own name, and the father will be called Senior (Sr.). Additional namesakes will take on the roman numerals III, IV, V, etc. It was once common for a man to change his name suffix from Jr. to Sr., or III to Jr., after his namesake had passed away.

Commerce and the American Automobile Association, among others. He was driven, competitive, and basically a workaholic. Mary's father, James Willard Maxwell Jr., pursued banking as well. He worked his way up to vice president at Pacific National Bank. He also continued his father's commitment to community service through his involvement with United Good Neighbors, which later became the United Way.

Mary's mother, Adelle Thompson, was a star basketball player and her high school's valedictorian. Her early accomplishments hint at her competitive and ambitious nature. She and James Willard Maxwell Jr. met at the University of Washington, the same place their daughter, Mary, would meet her husband years later.

Not long after Mary Maxwell and Bill Gates Jr. married, they moved to Seattle. Bill Jr. went into private law practice and eventually became partner in a law firm. Mary Gates put her education degree to work and taught school. But her overriding drive was to be involved with the community.

Mary Gates threw herself into the world of volunteerism and philanthropy. William P. Gerberding, past president of the University

Bill Gates (left) and his father (right) remain devoted to charity work.

of Washington, described Mary Gates:

> *She was a catalyst, a person who sought and often found common ground when it was not apparent to others. Everyone trusted her and respected her judgment. Her leadership was subtle, but it was steady.*[1]

Mary Gates served on boards of both corporations and nonprofit groups. She became the first woman to chair the King County United Way and the first female director of the First Interstate Bank of Washington. She was appointed to the University of Washington board of regents and served for 18 years. Her resume of community service is diverse and lengthy. In fact, she devoted so much of her time to these organizations that it often took away from family time.

### Inborn Drive

Bill Gates was born into a family of go-getters. In the late 1800s, his great-grandfather on his mother's side, James Willard Maxwell, pioneered his way from an Iowa farm to the state of Washington. He became a banker, the mayor of South Bend, served on the school board, and worked as a state legislator. He and his family then moved to Seattle, and his work in banking (he founded National City Bank) rewarded him with national recognition within banking circles.

Bill Gates's great-grandfather on his father's side, William Henry Gates Sr., moved his family from Seattle to Alaska to try to cash in on the gold rush fever. They lived in Alaska for more than ten years. Then they moved back to Washington state and started a furniture business.

Gates's great-grandparents could not have made it as far as they had if they had not been hard workers. It is no wonder that Bill Gates has such a pioneering drive—and such a strong work ethic.

## Gam

Mary and Bill Jr. had three children: Kristianne, William, and Elizabeth—also known as Kristi, Bill, and Libby. With Dad practicing law and Mom doing so much community service, Gam often took care of the three kids. Gam was Bill Gates's maternal grandmother. The Gates family was ambitious, but Gam was especially hard-driving and competitive. Gam had a major impact on Bill Gates.

The whole family enjoyed playing games together, but Gam was a serious player and she played to win. She pushed her grandchildren to read and to excel at all they did. From this push, Bill would come to feel that any game was a waste of time if he thought he could not win. Robert X. Cringely (aka Mark Stephens), a computer journalist, wrote of Gam's influence on Bill Gates,

**Guess Who?**

Games were so much a part of the Gates's family life that one was used to announce big family news. Bill and his sister Kristi were playing "hangman" with their parents one day. As they guessed the letters and built the words, they realized their parents were sending them a message. The words revealed that there was a baby brother or sister on the way. That is how news of Libby's arrival was announced.

> *At the heart of it all is a sense of competition fostered by his grandmother, and played-out in board games and family athletic contests. The single most driving force in the development of Bill Gates today or any day is his competitive nature. The guy simply has to win, and will do pretty much whatever it takes to succeed.*[2]

## Family Values

Despite all the boards, hospitals, and charities that kept Mary Gates occupied, she was an attentive and loving mother. She kept her household well organized and well planned.

One characteristic Bill Gates is known for, especially in his younger years, is his nerdy-looking clothes. Mary Gates can take some of the credit for that. She was so organized that she would choose his clothes. She even assigned a color scheme to each day of the week.

> "It was one thing to have Mom upset, but when Dad's upset, you just don't mess around. I was a kid willing to cause trouble and break any rules, but if Dad was intent on something, you just didn't think twice about crossing him. He had this quality of energetic leadership. He conveyed, somehow, without being too explicit, his high expectations of us. There was a certain gravitas to his statements."[3]
>
> —*Bill Gates*

Although they share a name, father and son could not be more different. Bill Jr. is a large, commanding man with a button-down look and a button-down personality. Bill Gates III is slight and disheveled. Bill Jr. listens fully before he responds, and his responses are careful and measured. Bill Gates III can be impulsive and argumentative. The two men do have some traits in common. They both have a strong work ethic, and they both believe that giving to the community is important. Much of that was fostered during their family dinners.

Bill Jr. was a typical father of the times. He worked hard all day and came home to a family dinner and good conversation. However, conversations tended to revolve around politics and other happenings in the community. Bill Jr. and Mary regularly invited the governor and other important business and civic people to dinner. The children were always included. These dinners may have first sparked Bill Gates's interest in business.

**High School**

One of his former high school classmates said of Gates, "If you had asked anybody at Lakeside, 'Who is the real genius among geniuses?' everyone would have said 'Bill Gates.' He was obnoxious, he was sure of himself, he was aggressively, intimidatingly [sic] smart. When people thought of Bill they thought, well, this guy is going to win a Nobel Prize."[4]

However, Bill Gates's argumentative nature seems to be his own. Maybe because he has always looked younger than his age, Gates felt he had to be loud and blunt to be heard. He has a reputation of being overly confident and bulldozing his way to his accomplishments.

Later, Bill Gates's first serious girlfriend, Jill Bennett, would say that Gates was a pretty lonely man who was sustained by the closeness of his family.

Bennett described Gates's relationship with and feelings about his family:

> *He derives major strength and support from them, and loves each of them intensely, more than they'll ever know. ... His family is one of his greatest assets.*[5]

So here is a portrait of a successful, well-to-do, and strong-willed family whose values embrace excellence, competition, community service, and loyalty to each other. In the middle of it all is Bill Gates. What was life like for him to grow up in such a family and how did it affect him? Some may argue that the real question should be, "What was life like for the family to have Bill Gates grow up amongst them?"

*William H. Gates Jr.*

Chapter 3

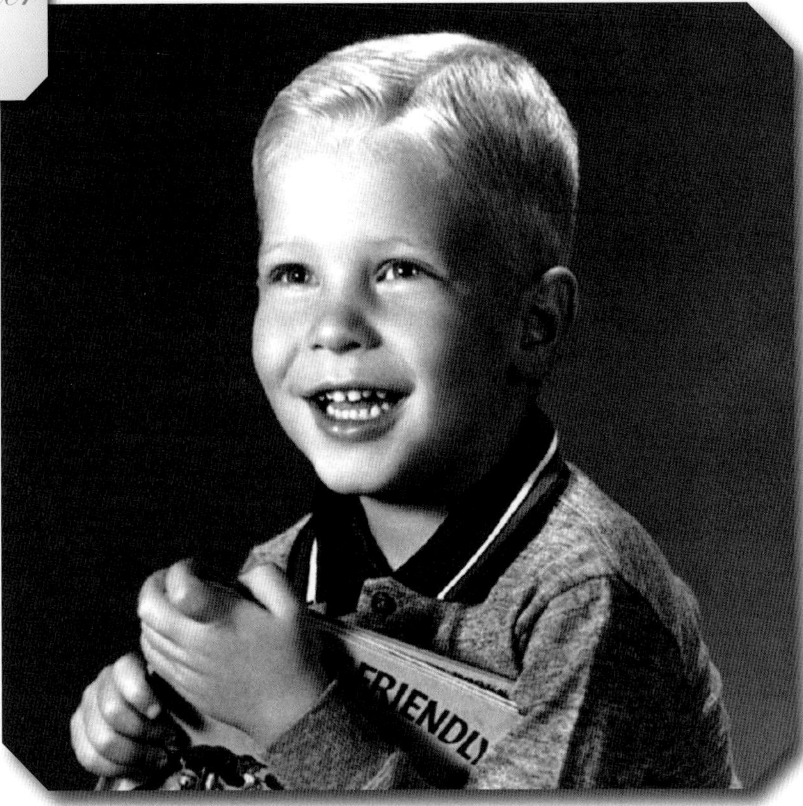


*Bill Gates, age 2*

# Trey

Bill Gates was born October 28, 1955, only a year after his sister, Kristi, was born. As a child, he figured out how to rock himself, and he rocked a lot. He still does. His favorite toy as a toddler was a rocking horse.

Bill Gates's mother stopped teaching to take care of her children. With more free time, she began forging her way into the world of charities and high society while still being a devoted mother. She brought young Bill with her to some of the talks she gave on behalf of the charities she represented. Gam lived with the Gates family and was always available to help with the house and kids when needed.

**Trey**

Bill Gates's grandmother taught him how to play cards when he was quite young. He was given the nickname "Trey" because of the III in his name. Trey is the card player's word for "three."

## Smarty Pants

Trey, as Bill was nicknamed by his family, was always one of the younger kids in his class. His small stature, his squeaky voice, his ridiculously large feet, and his nerdy-looking clothes made him seem even younger. He was also immature compared to the other kids in his class. Even so, young Trey's desire to be the best kept him at the top of the class academically.

His drive to excel was remarkable for a grade-school child, and it set him apart from everyone else in his class. He often did far more work than the teacher assigned, turning a small two-page essay assignment into a complete, in-depth, multi-page discussion of the topic. It is said that by the time he was nine years old, he had read every volume of the *World Book* encyclopedia from beginning to end. Some say he got distracted and stopped at the letter *P*.

Trey quickly caught on to subjects such as science, math, and geography, which he found interesting and exciting. His grades in these subjects, mostly As, reflected his interest. He thought some of the other topics taught in school, such as penmanship, were not worth his time. He got poor grades in those classes.

Trey was also motivated to get poor grades in some of his classes because it was considered girly to get all good grades. In one interview, he said,

> *I remember girls always got so much better grades than boys, so it was wimpy to get good grades. So I only got good grades in reading and math.*[1]

**A Challenge**

When Trey was 11 years old, the children in his church, the University Congregational Church, were challenged by the reverend to memorize the Sermon on the Mount. It took Trey two and a half hours to memorize the sermon, and his 25-minute recitation was flawless. He was motivated by the reward: dinner in the rotating restaurant at the top of the Space Needle.

## Playing to Win

Trey may have looked like a nerd, he may have dressed like a nerd, but when competing in sports, he was

Bill Gates (top row, center) played football in 1966.

anything but a nerd. Although he did not do well in team sports, he excelled in individual sports such as waterskiing and tennis. Again, his competitive nature would kick in—he had to win.

Trey spent much of his active summers swimming, sailing, and roller-skating. Each July, he and his family would spend two weeks at a group of cabins called Cheerio on Hood Canal. This is where he learned how to play tennis and waterski. Every year, all the families at Cheerio, 12 families in all, competed in a series of contests, races, and games. Tennis tournaments were held on Saturdays, and a variety of games referred to as the Olympics were held on Sundays. There were family skits, and in the evenings everyone gathered around campfires. At the end of the competition, award ceremonies were held much like those of the Olympics. The entire Gates family loved participating in those two weeks of all-out competition.

### The World's Fair

In 1962, when Trey was six years old, the World's Fair was held in Seattle. Its theme: Century 21. The exhibits were set up to give fair-goers an idea of what technology might be like in the twenty-first century, a good 40 years in the future.

In 1962, phone calls were made on corded phones with a rotary dial. There were no DVD players—or even VCRs. People were still watching black-and-white TVs. But the future was just around the corner. The first American had rocketed into space the year before.

So what were some of the out-of-this-world predictions? In Boeing's Spacearium, you could go on a make-believe flight to outer space. General Electric's house of the future had an electronic library and a home computer for paying bills, record keeping, and shopping. The IBM Pavilion had a maze you could get through only by making yes or no decisions that simulated how a computer works. Computers were exhibited that could translate words spoken into a microphone, and you could get hands-on experience by sending someone a postcard written on IBM's Selectric Typewriter—very cutting edge!

## Trouble Maker

Smart, young, and bored with his classes, Trey got into his share of trouble at school and at home. A strong-willed boy, he wanted to do things his way. For instance, his mother could not get Trey to clean his room. She eventually gave up and just required that he keep his bedroom door closed so she would not have to see the mess. Trey often dawdled and would stay in his room long after he was called to come out. Once, when his parents asked why he was not coming out of his room yet, he replied that he was thinking. Then in annoyance, Trey asked if they had ever tried thinking. They did not know how to respond.

***The Weekly Receiver***

Young Bill Gates started a local newspaper when he was 13 years old, *The Weekly Receiver.* Its sports section was known for its accuracy. Gates and a friend were even allowed to view local games from the press box.

At one point, Trey and his mother fought constantly with each other. Mrs. Gates thought Trey should do what she asked him to do, and Trey did not agree. Trey's parents sent him to a psychologist for testing and counseling. After a year, the psychologist advised Mrs. Gates that it was useless to try to win a fight with Trey. He was not going to change. Like it or not, Mrs. Gates had to accept that Trey's will would overpower her own. He had won again.

By the time Trey was in sixth grade, he was bored with school. He was fooling around a lot and getting into trouble regularly. Trey's dad thought his son needed smaller classes so he would get more attention:

> *We became concerned about him when he was ready for junior high. He was so small and shy, in need of protection, and his interests were so very different from the typical sixth grader's.*[2]

Trey's mother thought her son needed more discipline because he had been the one in control for the last few years.

**Lakeside School**

When the family visited Lakeside School for the first time, Trey saw that the students had to follow rigid rules. The jacket-and-tie dress code and the briefcase-carrying boys did not sit well with him. Trey threatened to fail the entrance exam on purpose.

Although the Gates family was well-off and could afford private schools, the past few generations had attended public schools. Trey's mother had even taught public school. However, Trey's parents did not think he would receive the attention and discipline he needed from a public school. It was a tough decision, but Trey's parents decided private school would be best for him. Trey was enrolled in Lakeside School, an all-boys college prep school with high academic standards that catered to Seattle's wealthiest citizens.

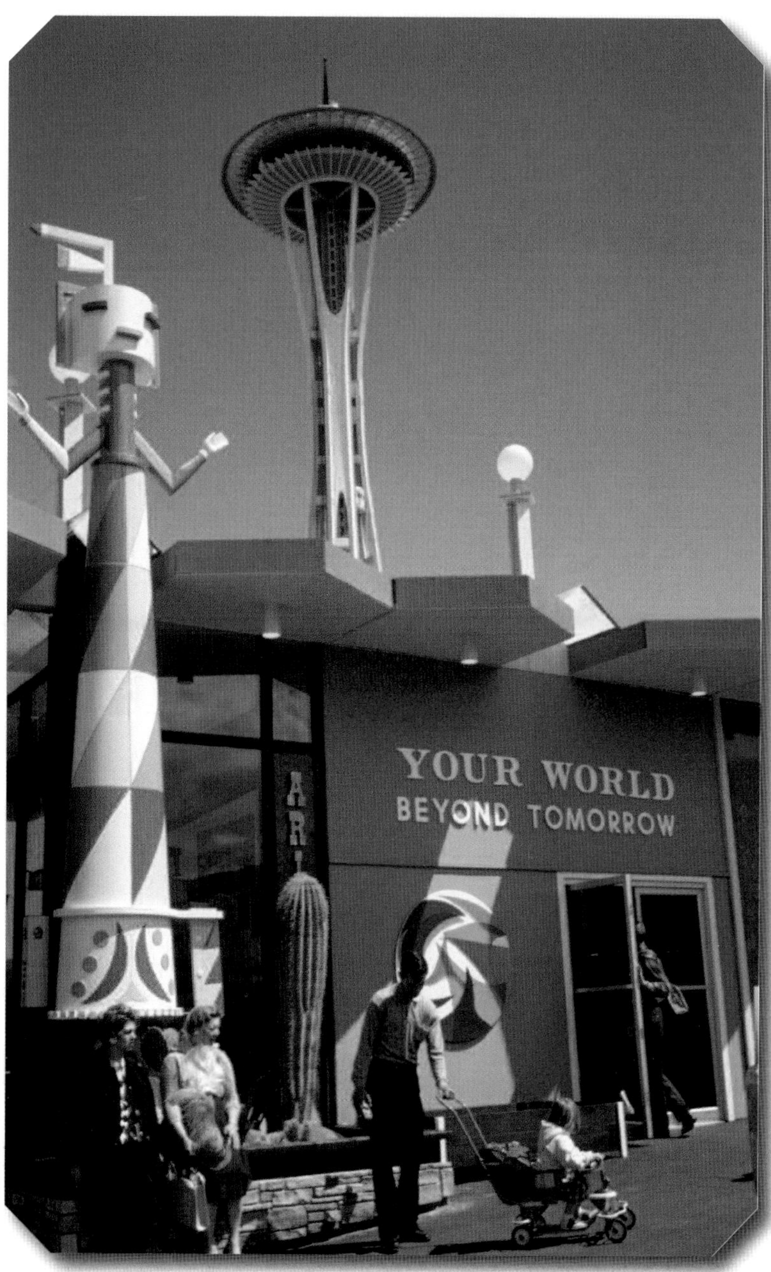


*The World's Fair was held in Seattle in 1962, when Bill Gates was six years old. It showcased technological advancements that were expected in the future.*

Chapter 4

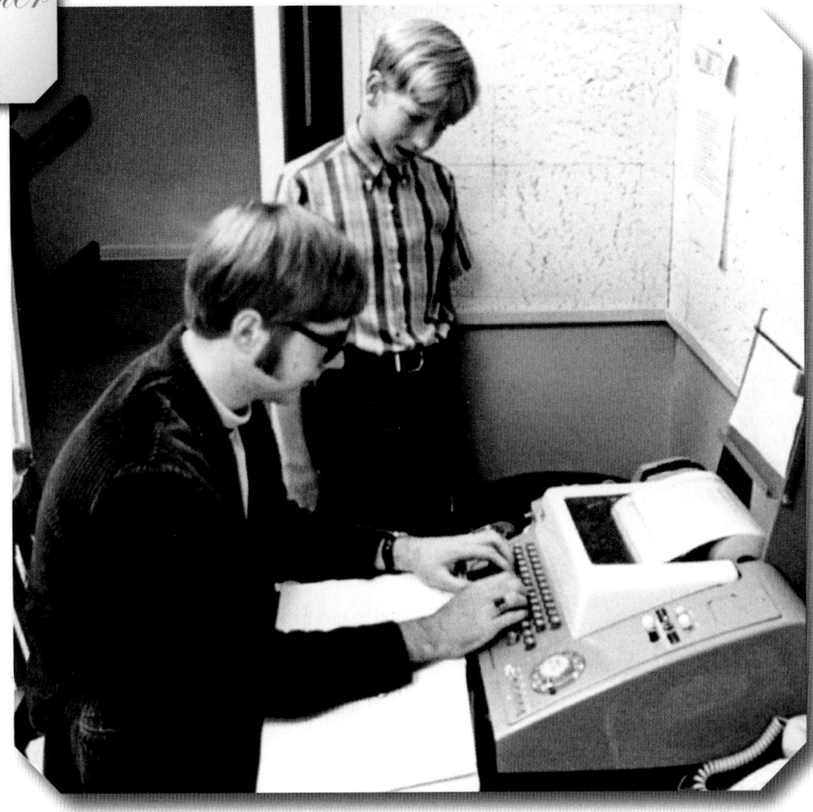

*Bill Gates and Paul Allen use Lakeside's teletype machine.*

# An Obsession Is Born

Seventh-grader Bill Gates entered Lakeside School in 1967, in the midst of a decade of great changes. The Vietnam War was causing social unrest. People were demonstrating against the war and against the social and governmental systems that were in place. "Question Authority" was the motto of the day. To young people, anyone or anything that represented rules was bad. In response, Lakeside relaxed some of the policies regarding personal appearance.

On the flip side, astounding technological advances in the 1960s were enriching people's lives. For instance, color TVs were starting to find their way into living rooms, and the space program was taking off. The first Americans went into space in the early part of the decade, and the first moon walk would happen before its end. Computers were making much of this possible. Lakeside decided to find a way to acquire a computer and introduce its students to this new technology.

The Lakeside Mothers' Club, a group of mothers who sponsored fundraising events for the school, had raised nearly $3,000 at a rummage sale. They decided to spend it on a computer. Most computers were too big and too expensive for anyone but governments, universities, and large corporations to own. The Lakeside Mothers' Club rented a time-sharing system. It consisted of a teletype machine, an off-site

**Apollo Guidance Computer**

In 1968, the Apollo Guidance Computer was used for the first time on a spacecraft. It rode on Apollo 7, which orbited Earth. In 1969, the computer went into space again, this time to the moon on Apollo 11.

**The Teletype**

The teletype was a mechanical machine, not electronic. When you typed on its keyboard, you would have to push the stiff keys down about half an inch. It was quite the workout for your fingers!

computer, and a phone line. Type a command on the teletype's yellow paper tape, dial a number, feed in the tape, and the teletype would "talk" to an off-site computer through a phone line.

## Learning the Language

When his math teacher introduced the class to the computer, Bill Gates was intrigued. He was also allowed to try it that day. Getting the typed-back response from a computer so far away was so thrilling that it ignited an obsession. Gates spent every free moment he had with the teletype. It did not take long for him to know more about computers than his teachers—about one week.

The computer was GE's PDP-10, and it ran on the BASIC language. It was called a time-sharing system because people from many different locations could use this PDP-10 at the same time. Every time someone dialed out to the computer, a connection fee, a usage fee, and a storage fee were charged. The Mothers' Club thought certainly they had raised enough money to last the year. Not quite—it took just a few weeks for the enthralled students to spend it all.

Gates read and reread the GE BASIC manual to learn the programming language. BASIC is a binary language, using only two digits, 0 and 1. BASIC was developed to simplify programming, and the binary system is the simplest processing system that can be used. This mathematical aspect of computers was part of what Gates found so fascinating. It was not long before he wrote his first program. He was 13 years old and, not surprisingly, the first computer program he wrote was a game: tic-tac-toe.

Bill Gates's thirst for computer knowledge could not be quenched. He studied anything he could find about computers. And he was not alone in this quest to know all there was to know about computers. A handful of other boys, all vying for computer time, could also be found in the computer room day and night.

## Lakeside Programmers Group

Just as the money was running out, Gates and three of his computer room buddies formed the Lakeside Programmers Group. The group consisted of Bill Gates; Paul Allen, who later cofounded Microsoft with Gates; Richard Weiland, who was one of Microsoft's first programmers; and Kent Evans. The group formed to find ways to market their computer skills outside of school. This is how they hoped to pay for more time on the computer.

At about that time, a Lakeside parent started working for Computer Center Corporation (C-Cubed for short), a company in business to provide affordable computer time-sharing. She proposed to the school that some of its students help test the computers—find any bugs—in exchange for free computer time. The boys were thrilled. They spent their Saturdays at C-Cubed, and soon they were going after school as well. Gates even sneaked

**The Math in Computers**

Bill Gates always excelled in math. In high school, he took math classes at the University of Washington. His time at school was split mostly between math and the computer room, which meant he basically ignored his other classes. Homework started being turned in late, classes were skipped, and the teachers noticed. One of the unique aspects of Lakeside School was that it recognized the ultrasmart, eccentric students and encouraged them to follow their curiosities. That is what the school did for Bill and the other boys who were focusing their energies on computers.

It is not surprising that Bill was drawn to both math and computers. Math and computers go hand in hand—you cannot know much about computers if you do not understand the math behind the programs that drive them. Lakeside's chairman of the math department knew Bill. He said,

> *[Gates] could see shortcuts through an algebraic problem or a computer problem. He could see the simplest way to do things in mathematics. He's as good an analytical mathematician as I've worked with in all my years of teaching. But Bill was really good in all areas, not just math. He's got a lot of breadth. It's one of the unusual things about him.*[1]

out at night to go there.

C-Cubed had "hired" four extremely smart teenage boys who were obsessed with computers. The boys wanted to know the computers inside and out. It did not take long for the mischievous and curious boys to cause the computers to crash (or fail). They also broke into the system and changed the files that recorded the amount of computer time they were using. Their pranks were discovered, and they were banned from C-Cubed for a few weeks.

"A child's impulse to make a toy do more is at the heart of innovative childhood play. It is also the essence of creativity."[2]

—*Bill Gates*

The time spent at C-Cubed was not all fun and games for Gates and the others. When they found a bug, they studied the code to help figure out how to fix it. Gates and Allen also took advantage of all the information they could find at C-Cubed. They talked to the programmers, gaining as much knowledge from them as they could. They borrowed manuals and pored over them. Gates said, "It was when we got free time at C-Cubed that we really got into computers. I mean, then I became hardcore. It was day and night."[3] Gates was so desperate for information that he even scrounged the C-Cubed wastebaskets.

**The Draw of Computers**

When describing the draw of computers, Bill Gates wrote, "I later realized that part of the appeal must have been that here was an enormous, expensive, grown-up machine and we, the kids, could control it. We were too young to drive or do any of the other things adults could have fun at, but we could give this big machine orders and it would always obey."[4]

Bill Gates was definitely not a one-dimensional person. Even as a teenager, the family discussions at dinners stirred in him an interest in business. He would just as likely be seen reading a business magazine as a computer magazine.

At C-Cubed, he got a dose of the downside of the business world. Gates, Allen, and the others had been looking for bugs and security holes on the behalf of C-Cubed for a couple of years. There were many problems with the software and because Seattle's economy was going downhill, C-Cubed went bankrupt. One evening in 1970, the furniture was repossessed while Gates and Allen were working on a program. The chairs they were sitting on were taken from under them. On their knees and typing as quickly as they could, the two boys worked furiously to save their programs on tape before they had to leave the building. Now what were they going to do?

*Lakeside's teletype machine "talked" to an off-site computer similar to this one.*

Chapter 5

Bill Gates in the computer room at Lakeside School

# The Lakeside Programmers Group

Bill Gates may have looked like a nerd, but he did not act like one. He had friends and a full social life. He liked to play jokes on people. In addition, Gates loved fast cars. After he turned 16, he could be seen driving a shiny new red Mustang.

When Gates's parents told him he had to keep away from computers for a while because they worried he was spending too much time with them, it was no big deal. He just read books instead. After a nine-month break from computers, Gates eagerly returned to the Lakeside Programmers Group. Since C-Cubed had gone bankrupt, the Lakeside Programmers Group had to find a different place to access computers. For a while, that place was the University of Washington.

## First Programming Job

In early 1971, the Lakeside Programmers Group's luck changed. They were asked by Information Sciences, Inc., (ISI) to write a payroll program. ISI was a computer timesharing business much like C-Cubed. In return for their work, the boys would get free computer time and a share of the profits brought in by their program. This was the first time the Lakeside Programmers actually received pay for their work.

**Favorite Books**

Bill Gates loves to read. He especially enjoyed reading *A Separate Peace* by John Knowles, and *The Catcher in the Rye* by J. D. Salinger. They remain among his favorites even today.

After a while, Allen and Weiland decided that there was not enough work for four people, and they kicked the younger Bill Gates and Kent Evans off the project. Later on, Allen and Weiland became sidetracked by another project and asked Gates and Evans to come back. Gates replied, in no uncertain terms,

> *Look, if you want me to come back you have to let me be in charge. But this is a dangerous thing, because if you put me in charge this time, I'm going to want to be in charge forever after.*[2]

Allen and Weiland agreed, and Gates and Evans returned to the project.

**Business Side of Computers**

When the Lakeside Programmers Group started getting paid for their work, they had to turn their attention to the business side of computers. Bill Gates explained, "... we found a company down in Portland, Oregon, with the same PDP-10 that let us write a COBOL program, a payroll program, a huge complex payroll program. I learned about labor reports, taxes, and all sorts of mundane things."[1]

## Traf-O-Data

Paul Allen graduated from Lakeside in 1971, but that was not the end of his collaborations with Gates. Before leaving Lakeside, Allen and Gates started their own company, Traf-O-Data.

In 1971, cities used traffic-counting boxes connected to a rubber hose that stretched across a street to analyze traffic flow. Each box contained tape and a hole puncher. When a car drove over the hose, the machine recorded both the time and volume by punching the tape with a 0 or a 1, the binary numbers used in computers. Then people would "read" the tapes and convert the information into English for city planners to interpret. Gates and Allen set off to create a computer program that would analyze traffic count and volume. The plan was to get the information to cities quicker and cheaper than ever before. This was the beginning of Traf-O-Data.

At about that time, Allen saw an article in an electronics magazine announcing the debut of the 4004 microprocessor chip by Intel. A year later, Intel came out with the 8008 chip, which could do a lot more than the 4004. Allen said,

> *That's when it hit us how Moore's Law really worked—that each generation of microprocessor chip was basically twice as fast as the previous one and that they got cheaper too.*[3]

Bill Gates scrounged up $360 to purchase an 8008 chip. The plan was to build a computer around this chip that would analyze traffic flow. Gates and Allen got their friend Paul Gilbert to design the hardware (the computer). In the meantime, Gates and Allen started writing a software program using a Washington State University computer as a stand-in for the 8008 chip.

Eventually, Traf-O-Data met with some success, pulling in revenues of $10,000 to $30,000 a year. The company shut down, though, when the federal government started to offer traffic processing services for free. Although Gates and Allen's first real business failed, they did learn how to develop software before a computer was even built—a skill that would come in handy a few years later.

**Moore's Law**

Before Gordon Moore co-founded Intel in 1968, he made an observation that he put forth as a rule of thumb. That rule of thumb is called Moore's Law, and it made him famous.

In 1965, while working at Fairchild Semi-conductor, Moore suggested that the number of transistors placed on a computer chip would double every year and that its cost would decline. (Ten years later, he changed his prediction to every two years.) A transistor is a switch in a chip that controls the flow of electricity. The more transistors there are in a chip, the more the chip can do.

It may seem odd for this simple-seeming statement to be credited for having such a huge impact on technology. Moore's Law has been behind the amazingly fast advancements in technology. Professor Ian Mackintosh, one of the leading silicon chip pioneers of his day, says of Gordon Moore,

> *The influence of what he articulated has been hugely significant. ... Practically anything digital has depended critically on the swift improvement in chip density.*[4]

## Co-ed

Possibly the biggest change in 1971 for Bill Gates and the other boys of Lakeside School was their merger with St.Nicholas, an all-girls school. The merger of the schools significantly increased the population of the school and the number of courses being offered. Up until that point, scheduling classes at Lakeside had been done with paper and pencil. The sudden addition of so many new students made scheduling by hand nearly impossible.

The school turned to Gates to come up with a program that would computerize the scheduling process. Gates knew there would be too many things to consider. This included which classrooms could be used when, and not scheduling academic classes next door to potentially loud music classes. He turned down the opportunity at first, but later accepted the challenge with help from Evans. They were to have the schedule computerized in time for the fall 1972 term.

On May 28, 1972, approximately one week after Gates and Evans started working on the scheduling program, tragedy struck. Evans, an unathletic boy,

**Gates's Schedule**

Lakeside School paid Bill Gates $4,200 for a computerized scheduling program. Gates fixed the schedule so that all the seniors had no classes on Tuesdays. He also arranged a class that was all girls and one boy. That boy, of course, was Bill Gates.

decided to go on a hiking trip with a group from the University of Washington. The inexperienced Evans tripped and fell hundreds of feet to his death. Evans and Gates had become very close friends over the years, and Evans's death affected Gates deeply.

Gates laid aside the scheduling project for the first month of the summer and worked as a page in the U.S. House of Representatives. When he returned to Seattle, he still had the daunting task of finishing the scheduling program. He asked Paul Allen to help him, and the two went to work. The computerized scheduling program they developed was a success.

## A Serious Programmer

Partway through his senior year, Gates was contacted by defense contractor TRW. The contractor was having major problems with a program that was littered with bugs. In its search for people who were experts at finding computer bugs, the names Bill Gates and Paul Allen kept coming up. TRW wanted to hire them full time to fix the program's bugs. Lakeside allowed Gates to miss the second trimester. Gates and Allen eagerly started their first full-time job at the TRW offices in Vancouver, British Columbia. In describing his work at TRW, Gates explained,

Bill Gates and Paul Allen did programming work for defense contractor TRW.

*This was a real-time data project, controlling the power grid in the Northwest using PDP-10s. It had reliability requirements way beyond what the PDP-10 could deliver. So, we were really pushing the state-of-the-art. It never met the full power industry requirements, but they did put the system on-line.*[5]

Gates turned a corner at TRW—he became a serious programmer. One of TRW's best programmers, John Norton, took Gates under his wing and helped Gates sharpen his programming skills. For the first time, Gates had someone who knew more than he knew giving him feedback and advice.

While working at TRW, Gates received acceptance letters from various colleges. He was not yet sure what he wanted to do after college, so Gates chose the school that had the greatest variety of courses and the best reputation—Harvard. That decision made, and with his work done at TRW for the time being, Gates returned to Lakeside to finish his senior year and graduate.

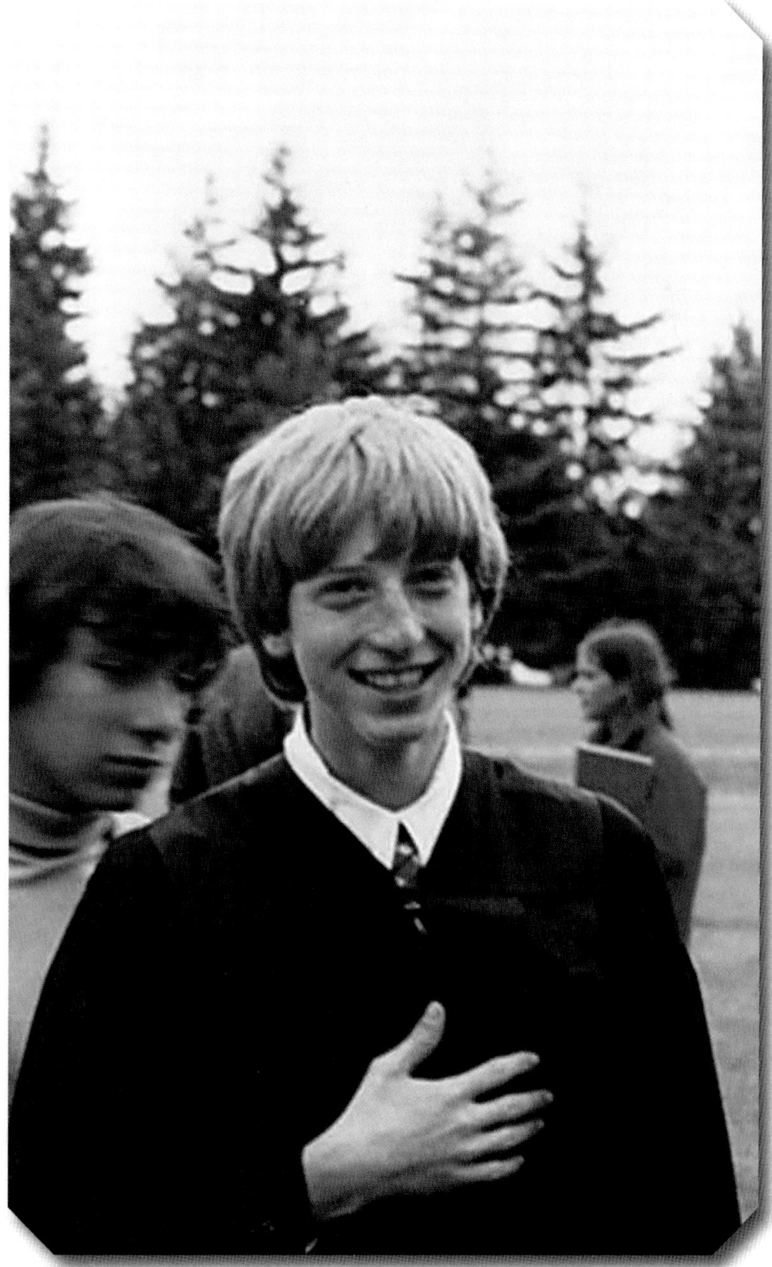

*Gates graduated from Lakeside in 1973.*

Chapter 6

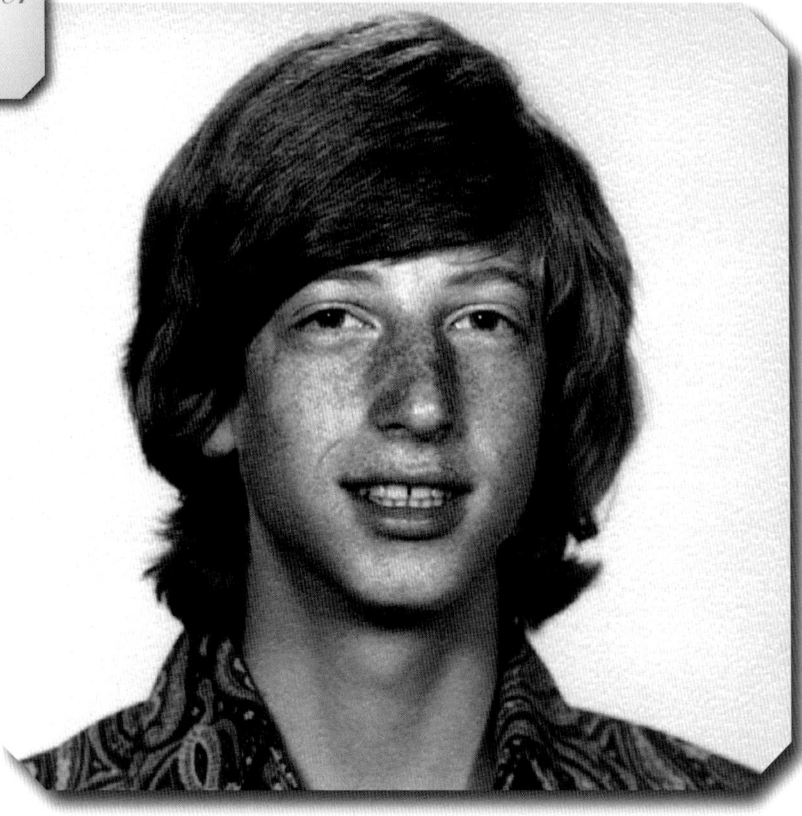

Gates, circa 1973

# It Works!

During the summer between high school and college, Gates returned to TRW to work with Paul Allen. The summer was not all work and no play, though. Gates still had his wild streak and still loved going fast. He and another TRW employee, Bob Barnett, would often go waterskiing. In between intensive work at TRW, Gates spent his summer having fun on the water.

Toward the end of that summer, Allen and Gates were talking seriously about starting a software company, something Allen had always been especially eager to do. But Gates knew how important it was to his parents for him to go to college. Starting a software company would have to wait.

**Waterskiing**

Growing up, Bill Gates loved to water-ski. He was extremely good at it. During the summer between high school and college, his waterskiing antics caused him to break his leg. He was supposed to keep his cast on for six weeks. Three weeks later, Gates returned to work without his cast. Although his leg still looked horrible, he convinced his friend to take him out waterskiing. Gates performed his most difficult tricks as though he had never broken his leg. It seemed his determination would overpower any obstacle in his way.

## Harvard University

Gates was more advanced than most kids entering college. He had already worked in the "real world," where he was getting guidance and praise for his programming skills. He had even owned his own company. At this juncture in Gates's life, he was feeling more confident than ever before. The potential of his future was obvious. Gates believed that he would become a millionaire in his twenties.

Despite his self-confidence, Gates entered Harvard unsure of what he

**Pickup Line**

Gates did not date much when he was in college. The couple of times he did date, he did not really know how to talk to the girl. His pickup line: What's your SAT score? Gates himself scored a perfect 800 on both the Math and Verbal sections of the SAT.

wanted to study. Economics, law, math—they all sounded interesting to him. Computer science was not on his list. He had been named a National Scholar by Harvard. Gates was just a freshman and did not know what subject he wanted to focus on. However, he was given permission by Harvard to take some graduate classes as part of his undergraduate studies.

As was the case in high school, Gates focused only on those classes that sparked his interest. Given his obsession with computers, it was not long before he found the Aiken Computation Laboratory, Harvard's computer center. Gates spent more and more time there. He even managed to use the room reserved for graduate students. Professor Thomas Cheatham ran the graduate computer lab, and although he admired Gates's programming ability, he was not a fan:

> *He's an obnoxious human being. . . . He'd put people down when it was not necessary, and just generally not be a pleasant fellow to have around the place.*[1]

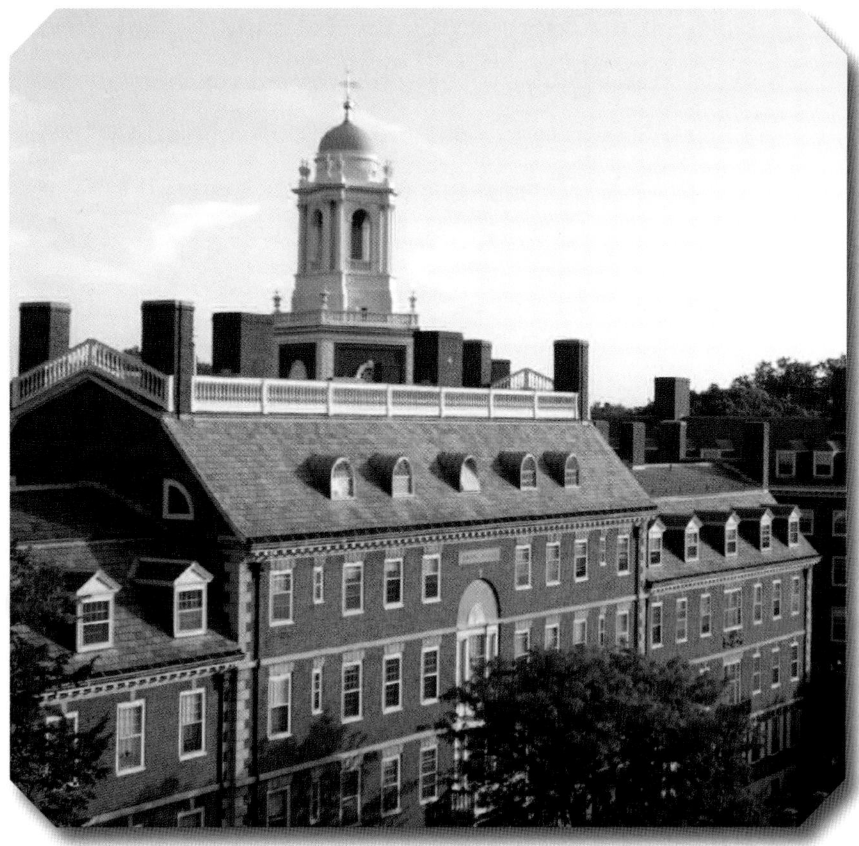

While at Harvard, Gates's main interest seemed to be developing his and Allen's business ideas.

When it was time for Gates to return to Harvard for his sophomore year, Allen was already working for Honeywell in Boston, Massachusetts. Gates and Allen had decided they needed to live closer to each other so they could focus on turning some of their business ideas into realities.

That year, Gates's dorm room was down the hall from Steve Ballmer's. They were opposites in many ways. Ballmer was large, outgoing, social, and involved in sports. He was studying applied mathematics. Although their personalities were different, they seemed to have some fundamental traits in common. They were both very intense people:

> *The two would often engage in heated debates, exchanging information at a high band rate like two computers connected by a modem. A short while into most conversations, Gates and Ballmer would start rocking in sync, talking at the same time but hearing every word the other said.*[3]

### The Intel 8080 Chip

An article in the spring 1974 issue of *Popular Electronics* announced the new 8080 chip made by Intel to control traffic lights. It had ten times the power of the 8008. It was just a bit bigger, but held 2,700 more transistors, and it was cheap—only $200. Intel and the rest of the computer industry saw the 8080 merely as an improvement on the 8008. Bill Gates felt differently,

> *Paul and I looked past the limits of that new chip and saw a different kind of computer that would be perfect for us, and for everyone—personal, affordable, and adaptable. It was absolutely clear to us that because the new chips were so cheap, they soon would be everywhere.*[2]

It was only a matter of time before computer hardware would be available to anyone who was interested.

In the fall of 1974, as Gates was beginning his second year at Harvard, he and Allen were putting their heads together to try to figure out what they needed to do to start a software company. When they saw the *Popular Electronics* issue with the Altair on the cover, they saw their opportunity.

Gates would later hire Ballmer to be his right-hand man at Microsoft. Gates's sophomore year was also marked by his new hobby—poker. Gates was not skilled at this game. He found he could use mathematic principles to help him in his poker games, but that was not always enough to win. Poker is a game of strategy made more complicated by the fact that players bet money. They also have to know when it is best to fold, or give up, a hand. Giving up was not something Gates liked to do, and it often caused him to lose. Despite that, Gates found poker almost as interesting and exciting as computers.

**Another Partner**

While writing the BASIC program for the Altair, Gates and Allen came up against writing floating-point math, an element needed in their program. Neither of them wanted to write this program. Monte Davidoff, a freshman at Harvard, overheard their conversation and said he had written that sort of thing before. Gates and Allen decided to include him in their project.

## The Altair Minicomputer

Things began to change with the announcement of the Altair minicomputer manufactured by MITS. This was the chance Gates and Allen had been looking for—a computer built around Intel's 8080 chip—a computer that needed software. They went to work writing a BASIC program for the Altair. In just over two months, their BASIC program was ready to be tested.

**Sophomore Year**

Looking back at his sophomore year in college, Gates said that he spent a lot of his time "being a philosophical and depressed guy, trying to figure out what I was doing with my life."[4]

Allen went to the MITS office in Albuquerque, New Mexico, to test the BASIC program. Neither Ed Roberts, the owner of MITS and creator of the Altair, nor Paul Allen really believed the program was going to work. It took approximately 15 minutes for the tape to be read by the machine. Then, the words "MEMORY SIZE?" came from the teletype. Allen typed in the memory size. Then the word "READY" appeared. He typed "PRINT 2 + 2," and the answer came back: "4." It works! Roberts and Allen were both awestruck by their success.

Allen returned to Boston with an Altair and a new job with MITS. He would move there in a month. He and Gates celebrated with ice cream and soda. They knew they were celebrating more than their success; they were celebrating a new era—the computer revolution had begun.

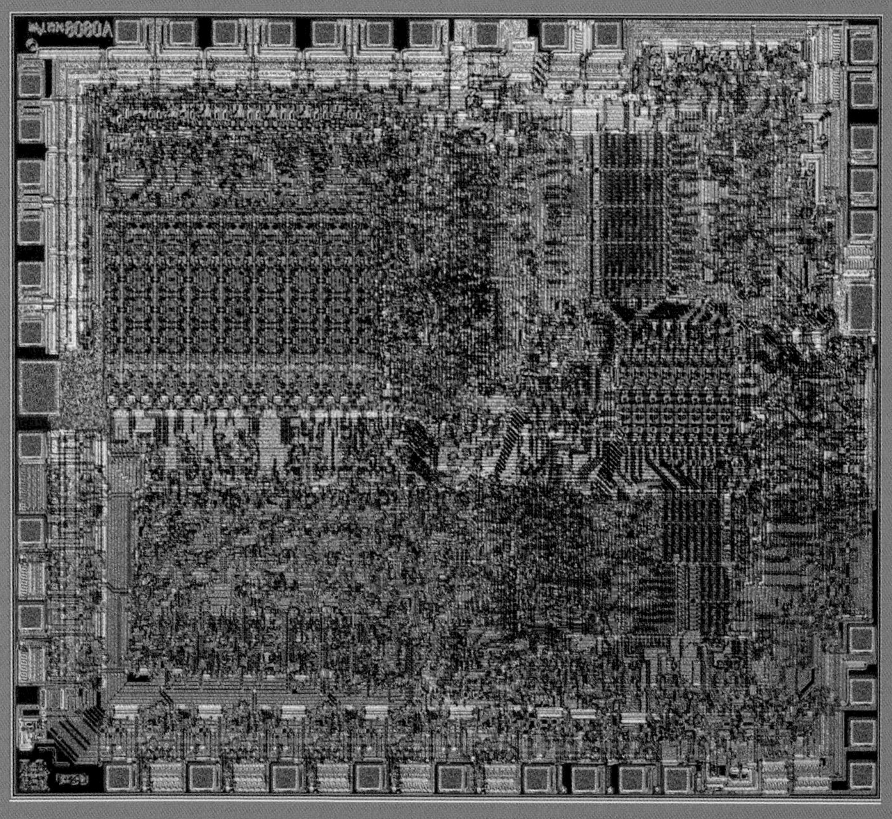

*The Intel 8080 chip was a key component in the Altair 8800.*

Chapter 7

*Bill Gates co-founded Microsoft with Paul Allen in 1975.*

# We Set the Standard

The Altair was selling beyond MITS's expectations. When people learned they could get the Altair with a BASIC programming language, orders really came in. The problem, though, was that although Gates's BASIC worked in the Altair, it was still full of bugs. And that work was slow going.

Then Gates came up against another problem. The Harvard administration noticed that he had been using the campus computer far more than any other student. When they looked into it further, they found that he also had Paul Allen, who was not a Harvard student, working with him. The two were developing a computer program for commercial use. This was not allowed. Gates faced expulsion. Ultimately, Harvard decided to give Gates a stern talk and left it at that. Gates was forced into buying computer time from a public timesharing service to continue work on getting the bugs out of his BASIC program.

## Starting Microsoft

With Allen in Albuquerque acting as MITS's software director, Gates started planning how he would tell his parents that he was going to start a software company in New Mexico. Of course the news took his parents by surprise, but eventually they came to terms with it. That summer of 1975, Gates joined Allen, ready to continue work perfecting Altair

**A Hot Idea**

MITS was near bankruptcy when Ed Roberts had the idea to manufacture a computer kit that would be affordable for nearly everyone. Even before the Altair was ready to be sold, MITS had received thousands of orders. The idea of a personal computer was so appealing that people were eager to buy the newfangled and untested Altair.

BASIC. They stayed at one of Albuquerque's motels. There, they came up with a name for their new software company, abbreviating "microcomputer software" to Micro-Soft. It did not take long for them to lose the hyphen, settling on the now-familiar name, Microsoft.

As the bugs were being worked out of the Altair BASIC code, the time had come for Gates and Allen to license the program to MITS. The license gave MITS exclusive world rights to Altair BASIC for ten years. It also allowed MITS to sublicense the program to other companies. Gates and Allen received $3,000 upon signing the agreement and royalties, or payment for each copy sold, from $10 to $60, depending on the type of Altair BASIC sold. A clause in the agreement required all companies using Altair BASIC to sign a secrecy agreement. The purpose of this secrecy agreement was to keep Altair BASIC from being copied. The agreement was not very successful.

**Gates and Roberts**

Ed Roberts and Bill Gates did not get along. Roberts thought Gates was argumentative and stuck up. That was the impression he often gave people. Gates thought Roberts ran a sloppy business.

## Pirated Software

To get people really excited about the Altair, MITS took it on the road

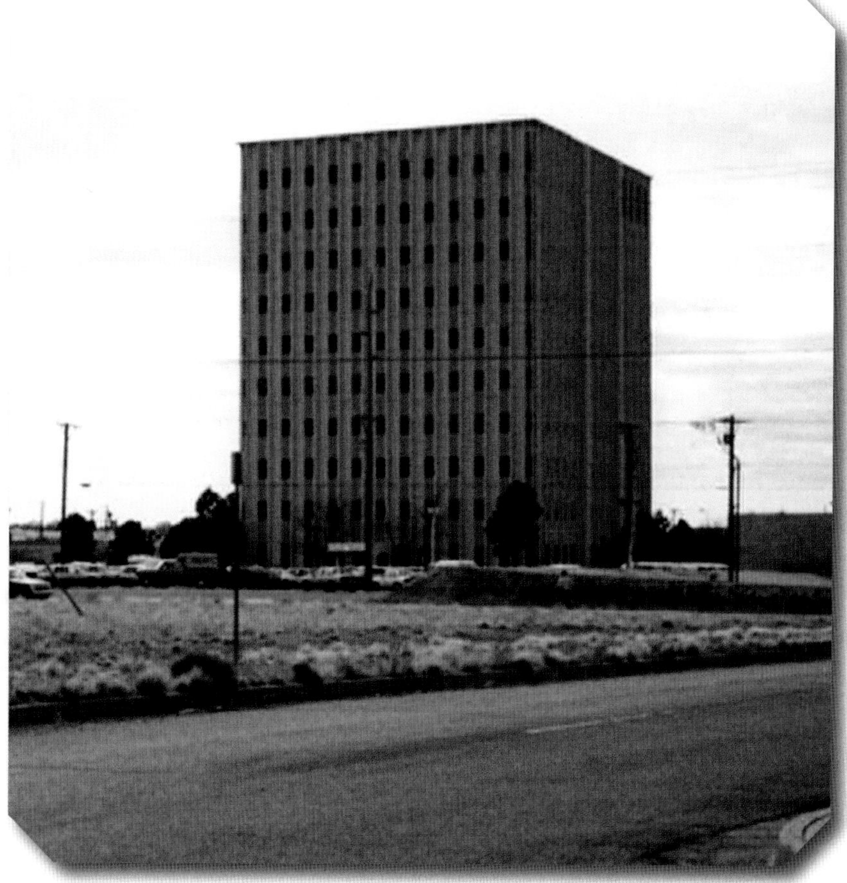

*As Microsoft grew, it eventually moved into Two Park Central Tower in Albuquerque, New Mexico.*

to demonstrate its abilities. Some people followed the van from city to city so they could see the demonstration again. Others came because they had an Altair and it was not operating properly—they wanted to get the experts to help them. At some point on this promotional tour, one of the BASIC tapes vanished.

Computer clubs were popping up all over the country. The people in these clubs were, for the most part, the people who were buying the Altair—and waiting for the debugged BASIC. Until they had the program, there was not much they could do with their computers. After the BASIC tape was stolen from MITS, copies of Altair BASIC began to show up on computers and in clubs throughout the country. People in these computer clubs were copying the program and giving it to anyone who was interested.

**Selection from**
**"An Open Letter to Hobbyists"**

"The feedback we have gotten from the hundreds of people who say they are using BASIC has all been positive. Two surprising things are apparent, however. 1) Most of these "users" never bought BASIC (less than 10 percent of all Altair owners have bought BASIC), and 2) The amount of royalties we have received from sales to hobbyists makes the time spent on Altair BASIC worth less than $2 an hour ...

Is this fair? One thing you don't do by stealing software is get back at MITS for some problem you may have had. MITS doesn't make money selling software. The royalty paid to us, the manual, the tape and the overhead make it a break-even operation. One thing you do do is prevent good software from being written. Who can afford to do professional work for nothing? What hobbyist can put 3 man-years into programming, finding all bugs, documenting his product and distribute for free? The fact is, no one besides us has invested a lot of money in hobby software. We have written 6800 BASIC, and are writing 8080 APL and 6800 APL, but there is very little incentive to make this software available to hobbyists. Most directly, the thing you do is theft ... ."[1]

Gates soon noticed that he and Allen were not getting very much in royalties from MITS. People had been copying Altair BASIC in greater and greater numbers. Gates was furious. He wrote "An Open Letter to Hobbyists," scolding hobbyists for stealing Altair BASIC:

> *Why is this? As the majority of hobbyists must be aware, most of you steal your software. Hardware must be paid for, but software is something to share. Who cares if the people who worked on it get paid?*[2]

There was some backlash with computer clubs arguing that copying Altair BASIC was no different from copying a music tape and giving it to a friend. The fact was, however, that the widespread use of Altair BASIC had made the program the standard software in the industry. People within the growing microcomputer industry needed the BASIC programming language, and they went to Microsoft to get it.

**The "Kid"**

When Miriam Lubow was hired as a secretary for Microsoft, she started working while Gates was out of town. When he walked in the door and into his office, Lubow panicked that there was a kid in the president's office. She could hardly believe it when she was told that the "kid" was Bill Gates.

## Microsoft Takes Off

With all its success and the new programs it was developing, Microsoft found itself in the position of needing to hire employees. The company was getting customers such as Intel and Motorola—the business was growing. Microsoft's first employees were Marc McDonald, a programmer, and Richard Weiland, as general manager. But Microsoft was not yet big enough to have its own offices. The four worked out of the house they shared. When Steve Wood and Albert Chu were hired, Microsoft rented its first office space at Two Park Central Tower.

**Workaholics**

Gates and Allen ran Microsoft much as they had run their lives in college. They worked day and night and slept now and again. Their diet was primarily pizza and soda. Every once in a while, they would go to the movies. Gates's favorite pastime was driving fast in his new car. It was used, but it was a Porsche 911.

Gates had been splitting his time between MITS and Harvard, but now Microsoft was starting to take off. He decided after the fall term in 1976 to take a leave of absence, in effect to drop out. At about the same time, Allen quit MITS to work for Microsoft full time. On February 3, 1977, Gates and Allen signed a partnership agreement, with Gates receiving 64 percent of the profits and Allen receiving 36 percent. Gates's share was larger because he had done more of the development work on their BASIC program.

A natural separation of duties evolved between Gates and Allen. For the most part, Allen did the programming at Microsoft and Gates handled the business end. Gates had spent a lot of time reading about all aspects of business. He learned about business practices and business management. He even could write and negotiate contracts, which saved Microsoft in legal fees.

## Parting with MITS

As Microsoft gained more customers, Gates and Allen's relationship with MITS's Ed Roberts became worse. The agreement they had for Altair BASIC limited Microsoft's income. MITS was supposed to license Altair BASIC to other companies, but Roberts did not stand by that agreement. Meanwhile, other people were developing their own programs, and they were free to market them to anyone.

Gates and Allen sent a letter to Roberts indicating that their license agreement would be terminated in ten days. Roberts fought this termination in the courts. During this time, Altair BASIC could not be sold until the legal issues were resolved. Microsoft was at a standstill and losing money. In the end, Microsoft walked away with all rights to its BASIC program. People had been waiting for the program for months, and Microsoft was back in business.

By 1977, businesses were adopting computers into their workforce at great speed, and they all wanted a BASIC program. Gates's philosophy was to sell the product at a low flat fee, and sell it over and over again to different businesses. By the close of the year, Microsoft was on its way to success. "We Set the Standard" became Microsoft's motto, and setting the standard had always been one of Gates's goals. He had reached it.

*Bill Gates compares computers from 2001 with those made 20 years earlier.*

Chapter 8

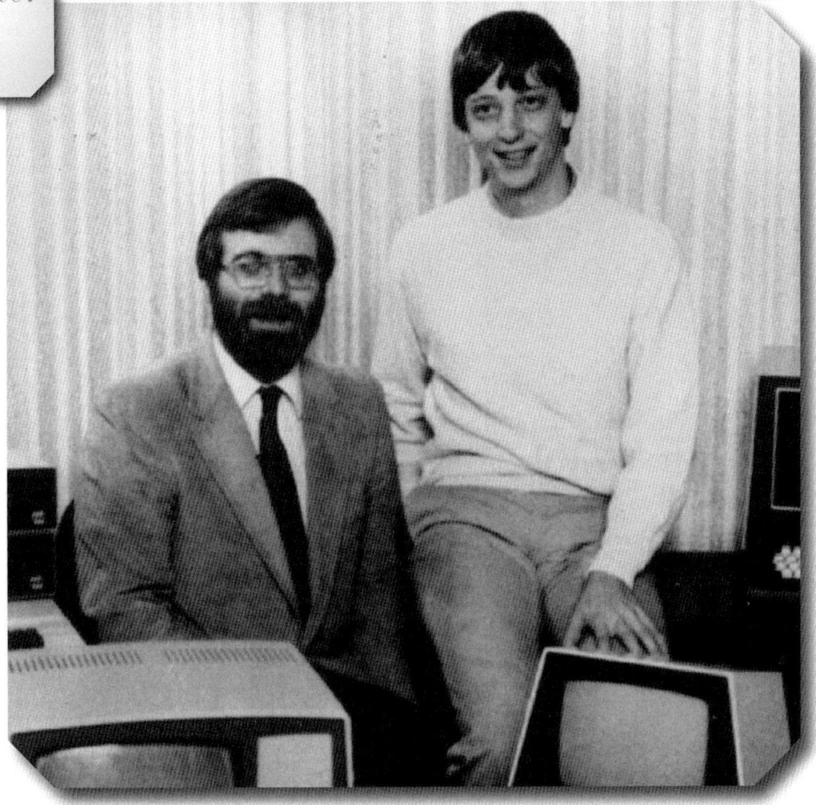

*Gates and Allen were excited by Microsoft's success.*

# A Growing Company

Although 1977 was a difficult year for Microsoft, Bill Gates did not stop having fun. He would often take a friend on wild rides in his Porsche in the middle of the night. He loved racing around curves and getting his car up to maximum speed. Everyone at Microsoft feared they would open the morning paper and read about his arrest—or worse. Thankfully, they never did.

## Larger Quarters

As much fun as Gates was having, it was becoming clear that Microsoft needed to move away from Albuquerque. It was hard to recruit employees, and business associates did not like to travel to New Mexico. On March 13, 1978, Microsoft employees received a memo announcing the company's relocation to Seattle at the end of the year.

In the meantime, Microsoft was busier than ever. Almost all the employees were young and loved what they did. They happily worked long hours nearly every day. Gates and Allen had never managed a company before, so their leadership methods were unusual. For instance, Gates used his competitive nature to inspire the other programmers with contests in order to get the type of product that he wanted. The office was run informally, with people usually dressed in jeans.

**Free Coke**

Bill Gates could not stand wasting time, not even if it was to eat or drink. It interrupted one's thinking process and it was time away from work. He decided to provide Coke to his employees anytime they wanted it.

Gates used a strange technique to challenge his programmers. He would loudly tell them that their program was stupid or that he could do a better job in less time. Work at Microsoft was intense and demanding. Gates's management style motivated his employees to go back to the drawing board and produce something better that would meet with his approval. If they disagreed with Gates, they were encouraged to argue with him. But Gates constantly challenged his employees and pushed them to do better; it came to be expected. Gates's emotional and confrontational management style helped improve Microsoft's products. His desire to be the best put Microsoft on the cutting edge of the computer revolution.

In December of 1978, Microsoft moved to its new offices in Bellevue, Washington, a city right outside Seattle. The suite was on the eighth floor. Bill Gates was the last to leave Albuquerque. He joined the rest of the Microsoft team a month later in January of 1979.

**A Rare Trait**

Steve Wood, one of Microsoft's first employees, said of Gates, "He can be extremely vocal and persuasive in arguing one side of an issue, and a day or two later he will say he was wrong and let's get on with it. There are not that many people who have the drive and the intensity and the entrepreneurial qualities to be that successful who also have the ability to put their ego aside. That's a rare trait."[1]

*Microsoft's small group of employees in 1978.*

## Twenty-something CEO

Microsoft's growing success did not change the flavor of the company. It was still an informal, casual place to work. At 24 years old, blue-jeaned Bill Gates still looked like a kid, and he often was not taken seriously—until he started to speak.

Gates was good at promising delivery of a product, but he was not very good at fulfilling those kinds of promises on time. Some companies resorted to sending their top executives to Microsoft to demand delivery of their overdue products. When they arrived, they were greeted by what appeared to be a disheveled kid. Their aggressive strategy would be thrown off when they realized that this "kid" was Bill Gates. Gates would launch into apologies and start talking about Microsoft and its vision. Invariably, Gates would sell them on a newer, bigger program,

### IBM

IBM (International Business Machines) started leading the computer industry in the 1950s. It was one of the biggest names in computers—so big that IBM came to mean "computer" to most people. It was so big that the federal government sued IBM for holding a monopoly in the computer industry. IBM split into several minicompanies, which significantly reduced their lead in the industry. IBM wanted to get back in the lead with an affordable commercial computer. The IBM plant in Boca Raton, Florida, had the task of producing such a computer.

So far, it had been innovative, scruffy, energetic young men, like Bill Gates, who worked on a shoestring, sometimes even in garages, who were creating personal computers. IBM, however, was a large company that was run strictly and by men in suits who did not encourage creative innovation. But the Boca Raton plant was given orders to do whatever it would take to create and produce an IBM personal computer. The strategy was to use available hardware to build the computer and outside vendors to supply the software. In July of 1981, Jack Sams of IBM called Gates to set up an immediate meeting. Gates had one month to come up with a prototype.

and the executives would walk away satisfied. Their product was still late, but Gates was able to get even more business from these companies. His salesmanship helped keep Microsoft afloat amid missed deadlines and poorly executed program designs.

**Calling Microsoft**

Microsoft's new telephone number in Washington was 455-8080. This number was chosen because the company had its start with Intel's 8080 chip.

By now, Microsoft employed 28 programmers and the company was still growing. It did not need another person who knew about computers, though. It needed someone who was good at business. Steve Ballmer fit the bill. In June of 1980, Gates convinced his college friend to accept the position of assistant to the president.

## Microsoft and IBM

Just one month later, IBM, the leading manufacturer of computers, requested an immediate meeting with Gates. Gates and Ballmer flew straight to Boca Raton, Florida, to one of IBM's plants.

That first meeting between Microsoft and IBM provided little information. IBM was strong on secrecy, so its representatives did not give Microsoft much indication of what it was planning. But it did lead to another meeting at Microsoft headquarters. At this

"IBM came to us because we were the common element of all PCs. If you took Apple, the TRS-80, the Atari, the North Star, the IMSAI, there was only one thing in common with all those PCs. That was, Microsoft had done the BASIC-language software on all those things."[2]

—*Bill Gates*

meeting, Gates was told that IBM was developing a personal computer. It was all top secret, so Gates was asked to sign a secrecy agreement. IBM asked Microsoft to supply the entire line of software for IBM's first personal computer, including an operating system. Microsoft came through within the one-year deadline. Best of all, Microsoft retained ownership of the software.

The IBM personal computer came out in 1981 with MS-DOS (Microsoft Disc Operating System). It was the first computer to use the 16-bit processor, and it was an instant success. Before then, computers were incompatible with each other. As Bill Gates once explained,

> *... Perhaps most importantly, this machine became the model. This was the machine that people decided to clone in order to build this base of total compatibility. ... And so by making the bus and the software and everything in here licensable by other people, they set up a thing that the whole industry could rally around as the next generation of 16-bit computing.*[3]

*Microsoft set the standard for computer software. The company and its young CEO, Bill Gates, made news.*

Chapter 9

*Gates topped the Forbes list of "World's Richest People" in 1995.*

# The First Billion

Microsoft continued to grow quickly. By 1981, revenues had reached nearly $16 million. The growth was also reflected in additional staff. By November 1981, Microsoft had moved to larger quarters in Bellevue, Washington.

## Microsoft Work Culture

Many Microsoft traditions made the move as well. Free soft drinks were still available for the employees, and every employee had an office with a window. Employees called each other by their e-mail names, which gave them a sense of being a part of a special group. Bill Gates's e-mail name was billg, so he was referred to as "Bill Gee."

Microsoft's success seems to be at least partially based on the smart people hired and its hardworking culture. Most people, including Gates and Allen, worked far longer than the typical eight-hour day, and most employees worked weekends as well. An amusing company quirk was its tendency to hire people who looked like Gates and who even acted like Gates.

Gates's competitive nature had revved into high gear by this point. Not only did he want Microsoft to dominate the market and establish the standard in the software industry, he also wanted to put his competitors out of business. He was well on his way to doing just that. A Microsoft executive said,

**IBM**

Before the PC came out, IBM was known for its business computers. IBM decided to focus its PC on business use instead of home use. From August through December of 1981, IBM sold 13,533 PCs—far more than IBM had predicted.

*Bill learned early on that killing the competition is the name of the game. There just aren't as many people later to take you on.*[1]

Microsoft experienced another type of growth. About the time when IBM announced its first personal computer, Microsoft graduated from a partnership to a privately held corporation with stock options. Only those people working closely with Gates received any of these stocks, which angered many of the long-term programmers. But they still worked as hard as ever.

Obviously, Microsoft was doing well. Gates wanted to do better. One of the areas of computer programming that he had been ignoring was application software. Microsoft had been focusing on system software, the software that operates the hard drive and that basically keeps the computer operating. Gates wanted to turn his attention to word processing software, spreadsheets, and other applications. However, other companies had been doing this for a while.

**Microsoft Stock**

When Microsoft first incorporated, the price of a share of stock was 95¢. Eleven years later, that stock share was worth $1,500!

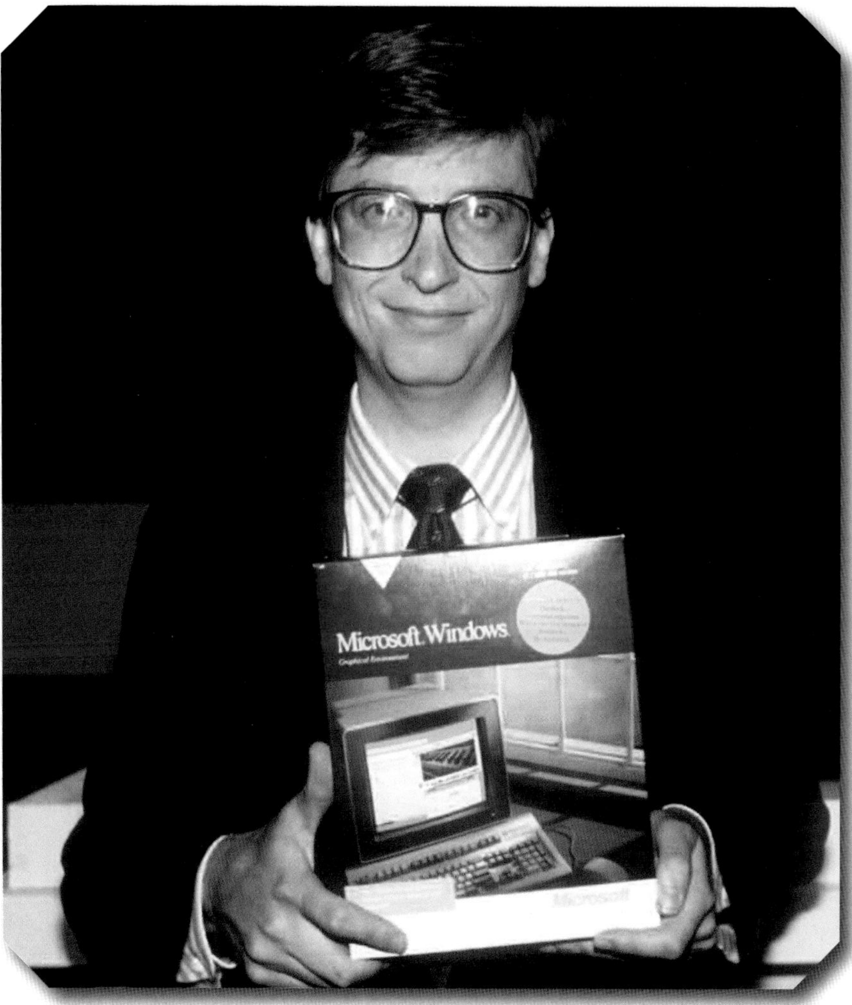


*Microsoft introduced Windows 3.0, considered its first successful Windows, in 1990.*

The additional competition did not bother Gates—he was still determined to rule in the application software market.

## Graphical User Interface

That summer of 1981, Steve Jobs of Apple Computers approached Gates about developing application software for the Macintosh. The Macintosh was another type of personal computer. The main difference was that it operated with graphical user interface (GUI). This means it used menus, icons, and a mouse to more easily navigate the system. Before GUI, computers only offered text and a keyboard. The Macintosh was to be marketed to the home user. Gates agreed to do the software for the Macintosh. He signed an agreement not to release software applications similar

### GUI

Xerox was the first to develop a computer with a graphical user interface (GUI). With its mouse, menus, and icons, the GUI made it easier, and more natural, for people to use the computer.

Steve Jobs, cofounder of Apple Computers, had already launched his first GUI, the Lisa. Microsoft wrote some of the software applications for the Mac and agreed not to release any similar software until the Mac had launched.

Later, after Microsoft launched Windows, which is also based on the GUI, Apple accused Microsoft of stealing its GUI. Gates said that was nonsense.

Bill Gates summed up the impact of the Mac when he said,

> *The Macintosh was a very, very important milestone. … It is hard to reconstruct, but people didn't believe in graphical interface. And Apple bet their company on it, and that is why we got so involved in building applications for the Macintosh early on. We thought they were right. And we really bet our success on it as well. And today, all of the machines work that way because it is so much more natural.*[2]

to those in the Macintosh before it was released.

Bill Gates had been introduced to the GUI by a former employee of Xerox, where it was first developed. Charles Simonyi gave Gates a tour of the Xerox facility and demonstrated the Alto. The Alto was the first computer to use GUI, and Simonyi had been one of the people who had developed it. However, as important as the Alto was in the history of computers, it was never sold commercially. Nevertheless, Gates was so impressed by Simonyi that he hired him to work at Microsoft. By 1982, Windows, Microsoft's GUI version, was in development.

**Losing Cash**

As sharp a businessman as Gates was, he was careless with his money. He once lost some traveler's checks on a trip to Australia and did not realize it until American Express called, saying it had found them. He would leave money strewn across his desk whether he was there or not, and he often lost credit cards.

## Life Changes

In 1983, Allen was diagnosed with Hodgkin's disease, a type of cancer that affects the lymph nodes. He left Microsoft to seek treatment. However, Allen was far from through with Microsoft. He continued to oversee Microsoft operations from his position on the board of directors until November 2000. After leaving the board, Allen continued to serve as a consultant for Microsoft executives.

In the summer of 1983, Gates met Jill Bennett, his first serious girlfriend. As smart as Gates was, Bennett saw that he was always worried about his business, and this kept him up at night. But during the day, Gates could fall asleep instantly. It was much like his college days. Eventually, Gates's work ethic came between them, but Gates and Bennett have remained friends.

Also in 1983, Gates bought his first house. It was located about half a mile from his parents' house in Laurelhurst. His mother and Gam decorated it while Gates was on a business trip. He did not do much to change the house. However, he did put maps up on the ceilings of the rooms, believing that the brain should be stimulated even during down times, when people are just idly looking around. He also installed a larger bathtub so he could read or otherwise conduct business while he soaked.

**Burgermaster**

A new tradition made its way to Microsoft's new offices. The company's building was next door to a restaurant named Burgermaster, which became the restaurant of choice among Microsoft employees. Bill Gates especially loved it. His near-daily meals of cheeseburgers and shakes won the drive-in restaurant the honor of being added to Microsoft's speed dial system.

## Focused on Success

Gates hated wasting time. Photo shoots for magazines and newspapers, even if they were good publicity for Microsoft, were a huge waste of time according to Gates. When he did agree to a photo shoot, it was often disastrous. He would often come unwashed, and his hair would be greasy. Shoots often took longer than promised because the crew was trying to figure out how to cover up his sweat stains or get an angle that did not show the holes in his clothes.

The 1980s was a head-spinning decade for both Microsoft and Gates. Windows 1.0 was released in 1985, and at the age of 31, Bill Gates became the youngest billionaire ever. Microsoft continued to experience strong growth, and it became necessary to move to larger quarters again. This time, college dropout, fun-loving Gates moved his company to a corporate campus. He thought a campus atmosphere would make for a creative environment in which to design groundbreaking software.

Gates describes this time in Microsoft's history:

> *But that same week we moved in, we went public as a company, this is our offering prospectus. And that was also the week of Microsoft's first CD-ROM Conference*

*where we were pushing the idea of multimedia back in 1986 that didn't really catch on, you could say, until 1994 so before it was in the mainstream. But this kind of shows you the pace of activity at that time.*[3]

Microsoft had spent its first 15 years blazing the trail to the personal computer. Its intent was to make the PC available and accessible to everyone. During that time, Microsoft developed MS-DOS, Macintosh software, Word, Excel, and Windows. Bill Gates's fierce drive to win helped put Microsoft at the top of the software heap. There was more to come.

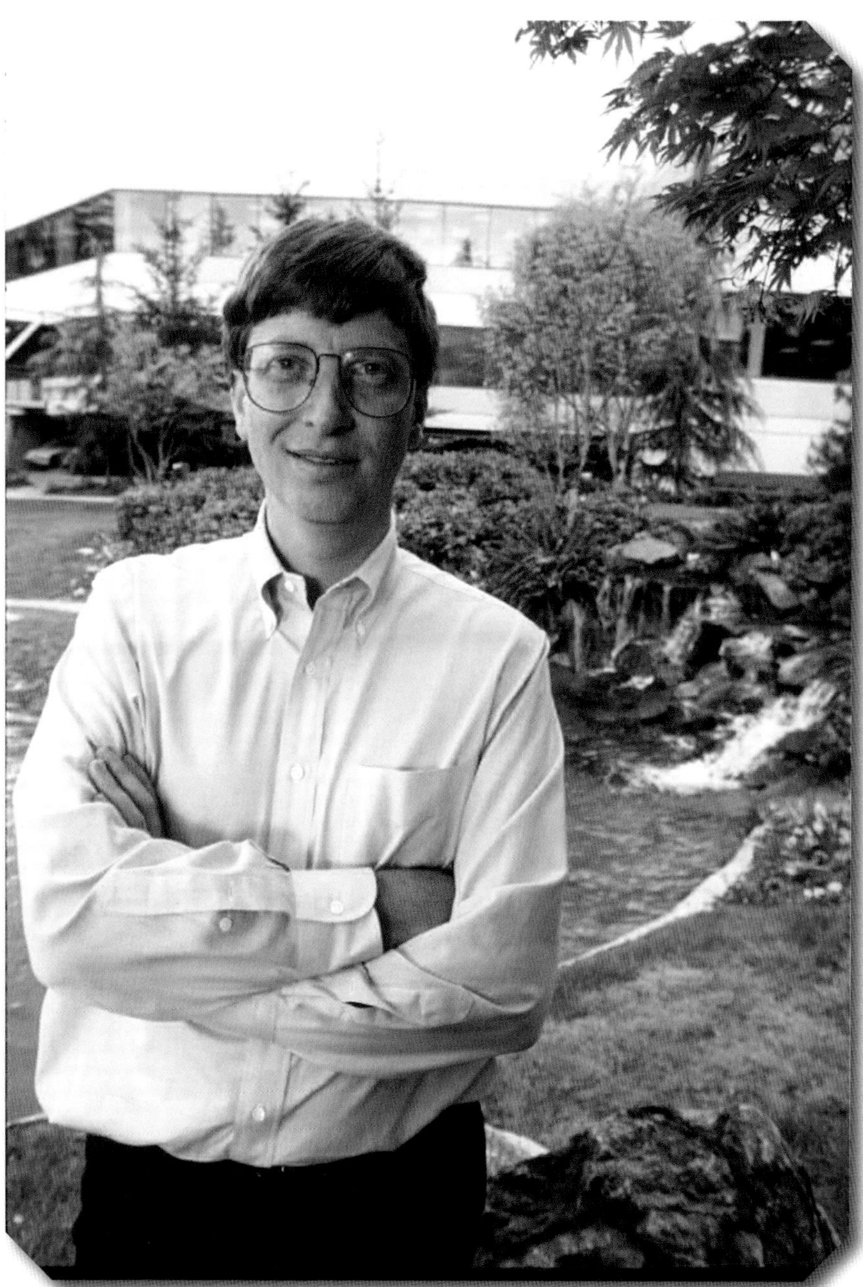

*Bill Gates moved the growing Microsoft corporation to a corporate campus.*

Chapter 10

*Bill Gates and Steve Ballmer at a press conference*

# Bill Gates Grows Up

In 1986, to honor his grandmother, Gam, who had recently died, Bill Gates built Gateaway. The four houses built on 3.5 acres (1.4 ha) were used as a family and executive retreat. Sometimes, Gates would hold Microsoft meetings there. Sometimes, he would go there by himself just to think. Harkening back to his childhood, Gates hosted an annual event in the summer that came to be called the Microgames. Much like his summers spent at Cheerio on Hood Canal, these retreats hosted team competitions and performances that tested the mental and physical skills of the players. The players were usually Microsoft staff members.

During this time, Gates was dating Ann Winblad, whom he had met in 1984. Winblad co-founded Open Systems, Inc., an accounting software company. Despite their common interests, Gates was convinced that he should not get married until he was at least in his thirties. He had noticed that famous scientists in the past did their best work while they were in their twenties. He did not want to distract himself during the years he would most likely be excelling. He had just turned 30 years old. He wanted to put off thoughts of marriage for a few more years because so much was happening with Microsoft. For one, 1986 was the year of Microsoft's initial public offering of stock.

**Still Friends**

Even after Gates' marriage to Melinda French, he and Ann Winblad would get together in the spring at Winblad's cottage on the beach. Winblad described those times: "We share our thoughts about the world and ourselves, and we marvel about how, as two young overachievers, we began a great adventure on the fringes of a little-known industry and it landed us at the center of an amazing universe."[1]

Winblad got tired of waiting, though, and the two broke up in 1987.

## A Computer in Every Home

Meanwhile, Microsoft continued modifying and perfecting Windows, their GUI operating system. In May of 1990, Windows 3.0 was launched. It is considered to be the first Windows success. Gates and Allen's dream of a computer in every home was coming true. Computers were selling at a rate of 20 million a year when Windows 3.0 was released.

Gates wanted to have a computer in every home, but he also wanted Microsoft to be the sole supplier of software for all of these computers. He wanted to squash all of his competitors. He wanted to win—and he had nearly succeeded. More and more of Microsoft's competitors spoke of what they called his bullying tactics to get new programs from them. While some believed his business tactics were unfair, others said he was a skilled businessman. These accusations attracted the attention of the Federal Trade Commission (FTC).

**Microsoft Stock**

On March 13, 1986, Microsoft stock was made available on the New York Stock Exchange. It opened at $25.75 a share and closed that day at $27.75. One year later, it was being traded at $90.75 a share.

By 1991, the FTC broadened its investigation of Microsoft. It wanted to determine if Microsoft:

> *... has monopolized or has attempted to monopolize the market for operating systems, operating environments, computer software and computer peripherals for personal computers.*[2]

The FTC dropped the case in 1993, and the Justice Department picked it up.

**Missing Deadlines**

Microsoft was famous for missing its software launch dates. It could be months after the launch of a program was announced before it was actually on the shelves, ready for purchase. This chronic tardiness was mirrored in Gates as well. He was often late for his speaking engagements.

On July 16, 1994, Bill Gates and Microsoft tried to settle the Justice Department's investigation by agreeing to stop what was being described as licensing practices that discouraged competition. But on February 14, 1995, the U.S. District Court rejected the settlement. At one point, Microsoft was ordered to split into two separate companies. But a federal appeals court reversed this decision, allowing Microsoft to stay intact. In the end, Microsoft agreed not to tie other Microsoft products to Windows.

Back at Microsoft, as advanced-thinking as Gates was, it seemed that the Internet boom was going to explode without him. That is, until senior programmer Ben Slivka sent a convincing memo on the potential of the Internet and the need for Microsoft to develop a browser. When Windows 95 launched, Microsoft Explorer had been integrated into the software package. As a result, Micosoft's browser became an industry standard. This practice was criticized because Microsoft Explorer's inclusion stifled competition for other Web browsers, which had to be purchased or down-loaded separately. Microsoft went to court again. The case was settled in 2001 and Microsoft

**The Dream House**

Bill Gates was still a bachelor when he decided to build his dream house in Medina on Lake Washington. The house is built into a bluff that is part of the 5-acre (2-ha) property.

The house is 40,000 square feet (12,192 sq m). It includes, among the usual rooms, a library, a theater, and a guest house. The property also contains a reception hall, an estuary, a boathouse, a pool building, and offices. Gates's love of fast cars required a 30-car underground garage to be built.

As one would suspect, the house has state-of-the-art technology. For instance, one wall is covered with 24 flat-screen monitors. Other unusual high-tech features are the electronic badges people wear in the house. These badges make each person recognizable to the house's computers. The computers are then able to adjust the climate in the room to that person's comfort level. Not only that, music, lighting, and the artwork on the walls are all personalized. The artwork is electronic, and changes in response to the information coded into each person's badge.

Gates spent approximately $50 million to build his dream house: a mere drop in the bucket for a multibillionaire.

agreed to have its business practices monitored by outside parties.

## Melinda French

In 1987, Melinda French had been recruited to work at Microsoft. She had graduated with a degree in computer science and had just received her MBA at Duke's Fuqua School of Business. She was a strong and independent young woman with a lot of common sense. She was only 23 years old. By 1988, she and Gates were dating.

Gates was 32 when he started dating French. Many of his colleagues were getting married and having children. People close to Gates wondered if he would ever get married. It seems Gates was thinking about marriage and family as well. He was in the process of building a $50 million home, and a children's wing was included in the plans.

Gates proposed to French on the weekend of March 20, 1993. Gates chartered a plane and the two flew to

**Children**

Before daughter Jennifer was born, Gates believed that the human mind was not unique. He believed that intelligence could be imitated by the computer's binary code. But with Jennifer in his world, Gates revised his beliefs, stating: "Analytically, I would say nature has done a good job making child raising more pleasure than pain, since that is necessary for a species to survive. But the experience goes beyond analytic description."[3]

Omaha, Nebraska, where they met with Gates's good friend Warren Buffett. Buffett had arranged for one of his well-known jewelry stores to open on a Sunday morning so that French could have the entire store to herself and choose her engagement ring. On January 1, 1994, Bill Gates and Melinda French were married on the Hawaiian island of Lanai.

Although Gates's mother attended the wedding, she was suffering from breast cancer and her health was declining rapidly. On June 10, 1994, Mary Gates passed away. Reverend Dale Turner commented on this difficult time,

> *It was a sad hour. Bill took his mother's death very, very hard. Bill loved his mother and she loved him. They were so close. That love helped to shape his life during his early years, and it blossomed in many ways later on.*[4]

## The Bill and Melinda Gates Foundation

Bill and Melinda Gates's first child, Jennifer Katharine, was born April 26, 1996. They also have two more children: Rory John, born May 23, 1999, and Phoebe Adele, born September 14, 2002. The couple had one more creation. In 2000, they formed the Bill and Melinda Gates Foundation.

*The Bill and Melinda Gates Foundation was established to reduce inequities and improve lives around the world.*

Both Bill and Melinda had been active with charities throughout their lives. They were also aware of the poverty and the lack of medical care and food that plagues much of the world. The Gateses were fortunate to have privileged lives. Now, they felt it was their responsibility to give back to society and try to better the lives of those less fortunate.

The Gateses believe that every life has equal value. They have created the Bill and Melinda Gates Foundation to reduce inequities and improve lives around the world. The foundation focuses on promoting world health and improving U.S. high schools and libraries. As of August 31, 2006, the Foundation had gifted $31.9 billion to charities.

On June 15, 2006, Microsoft announced that Bill Gates would give up his full-time position at Microsoft, beginning in June 2008. His plan was to devote himself full time to the Bill and Melinda Gates Foundation. However, he will remain a part-time employee and chairman of Microsoft. When asked about his days at Microsoft, Gates said,

> *I'd say that my job, throughout all this, has been, I think, the most fun job I can imagine having.*[5]

*Gates continues to be involved in the future of technology.*

# Timeline

**1955**

Bill Gates is born October 28 in Seattle, Washington.

**1967**

Bill Gates enters Lakeside School in the fall, where he develops his love of computers.

**1972**

Bill Gates and Paul Allen form their first company, Traf-O-Data. Gates sells a scheduling system for school, at the age of 17, earning $4,200.

**1975**

Bill Gates begins serving as chief executive officer for Microsoft.

**1976**

Bill Gates's famous "Open Letter to Hobbyists" is published February 3.

**1977**

Bill Gates and Paul Allen sign a partnership agreement February 3 to officially create the Microsoft Company.

**1973**

Bill Gates enters Harvard University in the fall.

**1975**

Paul Allen demonstrates the BASIC program he and Bill Gates wrote for MITS's Altair in February. It is the first computer language program written for a personal computer.

**1975**

Bill Gates and Paul Allen start Micro-Soft.

**1979**

Microsoft moves in January to Bellevue, a suburb of Seattle.

**1981**

Microsoft becomes a Washington state corporation June 25, with initial stocks going to a few insiders.

**1981**

IBM launches its first personal computer, August 12. It is run by Microsoft's DOS operating system.

**1985**

Microsoft announces the release of Windows November 21.

# Timeline

| 1986 | 1987 | 1990 | 1992 |
|---|---|---|---|
| Microsoft stock is made available on the New York Stock Exchange for the first time March 13. | At the age of 31, Bill Gates becomes the youngest self-made billionaire. | Microsoft launches Windows 3.0 May 22. | Bill Gates receives the National Medal of Technology from President Bush. |

| 1996 | 1998 | 1998 | 1999 |
|---|---|---|---|
| Bill Gates's first daughter, Jennifer Katharine, is born April 26. | The Gates family moves into their new multimillion dollar house in Medina, Washington. | Microsoft releases Windows 98 June 25. | Bill Gates's son, Rory John, is born May 23. |

| | |
|---|---|
| 1994 | Bill Gates marries Melinda French January 1. |
| 1994 | Mary Gates dies of breast cancer June 10. |
| 1994 | Bill Gates is named the wealthiest person in America. |
| 1995 | Microsoft releases Windows 95 August 24. |

| | |
|---|---|
| 2000 | The Gateses found the Bill and Melinda Gates Foundation. |
| 2000 | Bill Gates resigns as chief executive officer. He now serves as chief software architect and company chairman. |
| 2002 | Bill Gates's second daughter, Phoebe Adele, is born September 14. |
| 2006 | Bill Gates announces June 15 that he will step down from his position at Microsoft by July 2008. |

# Essential Facts

**Date of Birth**
October 28, 1955

**Place of Birth**
Seattle, Washington

**Parents**
William H. Gates Jr. and Mary Maxwell

**Education**
Lakeside School; Harvard University

**Marriage**
Melinda French (January 1, 1994)

**Children**
Jennifer Katharine, Rory John, and Phoebe Adele

**Career Highlights**
Paul Allen demonstrates his and Gates's BASIC program for the Altair 8800. It is the first computer language written for a personal computer.

Bill Gates and Paul Allen start Micro-Soft in 1975.

Windows 3.0 is launched in May 1990.

Bill Gates is named the wealthiest person in America in 1994.

**Societal Contribution**
The Bill and Melinda Gates Foundation was established in 2000. As of August 2006, the foundation has gifted $31.9 billion to charities.

**Residences**
Seattle, Washington; Albuquerque, New Mexico; Medina, Washington

**Conflicts**
In 1990, the Federal Trade Commission began to investigate Microsoft's business practices to determine if the company was monopolizing the computer software market. Microsoft has since been the focus of many similar antitrust lawsuits.

**Quote**
"I later realized that part of the appeal must have been that here was an enormous, expensive, grown-up machine and we, the kids, could control it. We were too young to drive or do any of the other things adults could have fun at, but we could give this big machine orders and it would always obey."—Bill Gates

# Additional Resources

## Select Bibliography

Andrews, Paul. *How the Web Was Won: Microsoft from Windows to the Web*. New York: Broadway Books, 1999.

Gates, Bill. "Interview with David Allison." National Museum of American History, Smithsonian Institution, http://americanhistory.si.edu/collections/comphist/gates.htm#tc1.

Gates, Bill, Nathan Myhrvold, and Peter Rinearson. *The Road Ahead*. New York: Viking Penguin, 1995.

Isaacson, Walter. "In Search of the Real Bill Gates." CNN. http://www.cnn.com/ALLPOLITICS/1996/analysis/time/9701/13/main.html.

Manes, Stephen, and Paul Andrews. *Gates: How Microsoft's Mogul Reinvented an Industry—and Made Himself the Richest Man in America*. New York: Simon & Schuster, 1994.

Wallace, James, and Jim Erickson. *Hard Drive: Bill Gates and the Making of the Microsoft Empire*. New York: HarperBusiness, 1992.

Wallace, James. Overdrive: *Bill Gates and the Race to Control Cyberspace*. New York: John Wiley & Sons, Inc., 1997.

## Further Reading

Brackett, Virginia. *Steve Jobs: Computer Genius of Apple*. Berkeley Heights, NJ: Enslow Publishers, Inc., 2003.

Lemke, Donald B. *Steve Jobs, Steve Wozniak and the Personal Computer*. Minneapolis, MN: Capstone Press, 2006.

Sherman, Josepha. *Charles Babbage and the Story of the First Computer*. Hockessin, DE: Mitchell Lane Publishers, 2006.

Sherman, Josepha. *The History of the Personal Computer*. New York: Scholastic, 2003.

Zannos, Susan. *Edward Roberts and the Story of the Personal Computer*. Hockessin, DE: Mitchell Lane Publishers, 2003.

## Web Links

To learn more about Bill Gates, visit ABDO Publishing Company on the World Wide Web at **www.abdopublishing.com.** Web sites about Bill Gates are featured on our Book Links page. These links are routinely monitored and updated to provide the most current information available.

## Places to Visit

**American Computer Museum**
2304 North 7th Avenue, Suite B, Bozeman, MT 59715
406-582-1288
www.compustory.com
Visitors can tour the museum and its exhibits. Dozens of mainframe computers and office equipment are on display. Presents 20,000 years of computing history in a timeline fashion.

**The Microsoft Visitor Center**
4420 148th Avenue NE, Building 127, Redmond, WA 98052-5145
425-703-6214
www.microsoft.com/about/companyinformation/visitorcenter/default.mspx
Visitors can explore the products and history of Microsoft. Exhibits display the latest in Microsoft's technology as well as the original personal computer.

**The Tech Museum of Innovation**
201 South Market Street, San Jose, CA 95113
408-294-TECH
www.thetech.org/info/
This science museum offers hands-on exhibits. Visitors can experience the latest in technology.

# Glossary

**algorithm**
A set of instructions used for solving a problem in a limited number of steps.

**antitrust**
Laws that protect companies from unlawful restraints, monopolies, or unfair business practices.

**BASIC**
(beginner's all-purpose symbolic instruction code) A simplified high-level language used for programming a computer.

**binary**
A number system with two as its base, each number is expressed by using only two digits: 0 and 1.

**bug**
An unexpected defect or imperfection in a machine or a computer program.

**code**
A binary system that translates information into a form that a computer can use.

**FORTRAN**
(formula translation) The earliest high-level computer programming language using algebraic formulas used for scientific applications.

**FTC**
(Federal Trade Comission) Federal agency that pursues fair competition in the marketplace.

**GUI**
(graphical user interface) Pronounced "gooey"; a computer program that uses menus or groups of icons to allow the user to interact easily with the computer.

**hardware**
The physical component(s) of a computer or computer system.

**lymph node**
A small swelling in the lymphatic system that filters lymph.

**microchip**
Tiny electronic component and its connections that are produced in or on a small slice of material, often silicon; data processor.

**microprocessor chip**
The brain of a computer; a chip that contains the elements for performing calculations and carrying out stored instructions.

**PDP**
(program data processor) Manufactured by Digital Equipment Corporation; a large, expensive computer connected to several smaller terminals that made timesharing possible.

**program**
A sequence of coded instructions that indicates the computer which operations it needs to perform.

**repossess**
To take something back from the owner as a form of payment.

**software**
The program(s) used in a computer or a computer system.

**teletype**
A typewriter-like printing device that was used to send and receive signals by telephone.

**transistor**
A switch in a microchip that controls the flow of electricity.

# Source Notes


**Chapter 1. Project Breakthrough**

1. "Microsoft's Tradition of Innovation: From Revolution to Evolution," Microsoft Corporation. 20 Dec. 2006 <http://www.microsoft.com/about/companyinformation/ourbusinesses/profile.asp>.

2. Harry Dweighter [Jacob E. Goodman]. "Problem E2569." *American Mathematical Monthly* 82 (1975): 1010.

3. "BASIC: A Manual for BASIC, the Elementary Algebraic Language Designed for Use with the Dartmouth Time Sharing System." The Trustees of Dartmouth College, 20 Dec. 2006 <http://www.bitsavers.org/pdf/dartmouth/BASIC_Oct64.pdf>.

**Chapter 2. The People Who Shaped the Man**

1. "About Mary Maxwell Gates." Mary Gates Endowment for Students Office of Undergraduate Education at the University of Washington, 20 Dec. 2006 <http://www.washington.edu/oue/mge/about_marygates.shtml>.

2. Robert X. Cringely [Mark Stephens]. "The New New Bill Gates: A Revisionist Look at the Richest Man on Earth." PBS. 20 Dec. 2006 <http://www.pbs.org/cringely/pulpit/2000/pulpit_20001123_000672.html>.

3. Paula Block. "Principled & Pragmatic: As Activist, Volunteer and Dad, William Gates Sr. Leads by Doing." *Seattle Times*. 26 Oct. 2003, 20 Dec. 2006 <http://seattletimes.nwsource.com/pacificnw/2003/0126/cover.html>.

4. James Wallace and Jim Erickson. *Hard Drive: Bill Gates and the Making of the Microsoft Empire*. New York: HarperBusiness, 1992. 37.

5. Ibid. 273.

**Chapter 3. Trey**

1. Stephen Manes and Paul Andrews. *Gates: How Microsoft's Mogul Reinvented an Industry—and Made Himself the Richest Man in America*. New York: Simon & Schuster, 1994. 18.

2. Walter Isaacson. "In Search of the Real Bill Gates." CNN. 20 Dec. 2006 <http://www.cnn.com/ALLPOLITICS/1996/analysis/time/9701/13/main.html>.

**Chapter 4. An Obsession Is Born**

1. James Wallace and Jim Erickson. *Hard Drive: Bill Gates and the Making of the Microsoft Empire.* New York: HarperBusiness, 1992. 23–24.

2. Bill Gates, Nathan Myhrvold, and Peter Rinearson. *The Road Ahead.* New York: Viking Penguin, 1995. 2.

3. James Wallace and Jim Erickson. *Hard Drive: Bill Gates and the Making of the Microsoft Empire.* New York: HarperBusiness, 1992. 30.

4. Bill Gates, Nathan Myhrvold, and Peter Rinearson. *The Road Ahead.* New York: Viking Penguin, 1995. 2.

**Chapter 5. The Lakeside Programmers Group**

1. Bill Gates. "Interview with David Allison." National Museum of American History, Smithsonian Institution, 20 Dec. 2006 <http://americanhistory.si.edu/collections/comphist/gates.htm#tc1>.

2. Ibid.

3. Bill Gates and Paul Allen. "Bill Gates & Paul Allen Talk." By Brent Schlender. *Fortune*. 2 Oct. 1995. CNNMoney.com, 20 Dec. 2006 <http://money.cnn.com/magazines/fortune/fortune_archive/1995/10/02/206528/index.htm>.

4. Jo Twist. "Law That Has Driven Digital Life." BBC News. 18 Apr. 2005. 20 Dec. 2006 <http://news.bbc.co.uk/2/hi/science/nature/4449711.stm>.

## Source Notes Continued

5. Bill Gates. "Interview with David Allison." National Museum of American History, Smithsonian Institution, 20 Dec. 2006 <http://americanhistory.si.edu/collections/comphist/gates.htm#tc1>.

**Chapter 6. It Works!**

1. Stephen Manes and Paul Andrews. *Gates: How Microsoft's Mogul Reinvented an Industry—and Made Himself the Richest Man in America*. New York: Simon & Schuster, 1994. 58.

2. Bill Gates, Nathan Myhrvold, and Peter Rinearson. *The Road Ahead*. New York: Viking Penguin, 1995. 15.

3. James Wallace and Jim Erickson. *Hard Drive: Bill Gates and the Making of the Microsoft Empire.* New York: HarperBusiness, 1992. 63.

4. Ibid. 61.

**Chapter 7. We Set the Standard**

1. Stephen Manes, and Paul Andrews. *Gates: How Microsoft's Mogul Reinvented an Industry—and Made Himself the Richest Man in America*. New York: Simon & Schuster, 1994. 91–92.

2. Ibid.

**Chapter 8. A Growing Company**

1. James Wallace and Jim Erickson. *Hard Drive: Bill Gates and the Making of the Microsoft Empire.* New York: HarperBusiness, 1992. 129.

2. Bill Gates. "Gates Talks." *U.S. News & World Report*. 20 Aug. 2001. 20 Dec. 2006 <http://www.usnews.com/usnews/biztech/gatesivu.htm>.

3. Bill Gates. "Interview with David Allison." National Museum of American History, Smithsonian Institution. 20 Dec. 2006 <http://americanhistory.si.edu/collections/comphist/gates.htm#tc1>.

**Chapter 9. The First Billion**

1. James Wallace and Jim Erickson. *Hard Drive: Bill Gates and the Making of the Microsoft Empire.* New York: HarperBusiness, 1992. 211.

2. Bill Gates. "Interview with David Allison." National Museum of American History, Smithsonian Institution. 20 Dec. 2006 <http://americanhistory.si.edu/collections/comphist/gates.htm#tc1>.

3. Ibid.

**Chapter 10. Bill Gates Grows Up**

1. Walter Isaacson. "In Search of the Real Bill Gates," CNN. 20, Dec. 2006 <http://www.cnn.com/ALLPOLITICS/1996/analysis/time/9701/13/main.html>.

2. Stephen Manes and Paul Andrews. *Gates: How Microsoft's Mogul Reinvented an Industry—and Made Himself the Richest Man in America.* New York: Simon & Schuster, 1994. 419.

3. Walter Isaacson. "In Search of the Real Bill Gates," CNN. 20 Dec. 2006. <http://www.cnn.com/ALLPOLITICS/1996/analysis/time/9701/13/main4.html>.

4. James Wallace. *Overdrive: Bill Gates and the Race to Control Cyberspace.* New York: John Wiley & Sons, Inc., 1997. 144–145.

5. Bill Gates. "Interview with David Allison." National Museum of American History, Smithsonian Institution. 20 Dec. 2006 <http://americanhistory.si.edu/collections/comphist/gates.htm#tc1>.

# Index

## About the Author

Ruth Strother is an editor and writer specializing in nonfiction books for children. She is the author of 11 books, including *My Pet Dog*, which was nominated for the 2000 ASPCA Henry Bergh Children's Book Award, the YALSA/ALA Quick Picks for Reluctant Young Adult Readers 2002 list, and chosen as an Outstanding Book on the Children's Book Committee at Bank Street College Best Children's Books of the Year list 2002. She lives in Southern California with her husband, her daughter, and her two Labs.

## Photo Credits

AP Images, cover, 13, 47, 58, 76; Seth Wenig/AP Images, 3; Heinz Nixdorf Museumsforum/AP Images, 6; John Froschauer/AP Images, 14; Andy Rogers/AP Images, 17, 99 (top); Greg Baker/AP Images, 23; Courtesy of the Microsoft Archives, 24, 27, 49, 50, 61, 68, 71, 96 (right); Ted Spiegel/Corbis, 31, 96 (top); Courtesy of the Microsoft Archives and Lakeside School, 32, 40; Jim McKnight/AP Images, 39; William B. Plowman/Stringer/Getty Images, 53, 97 (left); Michael W. Davidson at Florida State University, 57; Paul Sakuma/AP Images, 67; Time Life Pictures/Getty Images, 75; Carol Halebian/Liaison/Getty Images, 79, 97 (right); Dirck Halstead/Liaison/Getty Images, 85; Elaine Thompson/AP Images, 86, 98; Ed Bailey/AP Images, 93, 99 (bottom); EFE, J. L. Cereijido/AP Images, 95.